young muslim *voices*

Volume 9

Writings by
Participants of the
2017-2019
Essay Panel Contests

Published by Mafiq Foundation
Silver Spring, Maryland

ISBN-13: 978-0-9700372-6-8
Printed in the United States of America

Publisher
Mafiq Foundation, Inc.
P. O. Box 4916
Silver Spring, Maryland 20914-4916
U. S. A.
Tel: 301-928-3335
Website: http://epc.mafiq.org

Contents

Essay Panel Contests

2017 – Prince George's Muslim Association, Lanham, Md.
2018 – Diyanet Center of America, Lanham, Md.
2019 – ADAMS Center, Sterling, Va.

2017: Faith in Action: What does Surah al-Ma'un mean to me?

Elementary School

2017: Faith in Action: How should I serve my community?

Middle School

2017: Faith in Action: How can I address today's social challenges?

High School through College

2018: I Am a Muslim: What does it mean to be a Muslim?

Elementary School

2018: I Am a Muslim: How does being a Muslim affect me?

Middle School

2018: I Am a Muslim: How do we keep the flame of faith alive?
High School through College

2019: Civility, Ethics & Morality: Which moral values have I learned?
Elementary School

2019: Civility, Ethics & Morality: What does morality in Islam mean to me?
Middle School

2019: Civility, Ethics & Morality: How can I promote Islamic teachings?
High School through College

Dedicated to the students, parents, and organizers that work so hard to make the Essay Panel Contest possible, and to the Muslim community as a whole. May Allah (SWT) reward you immensely for your hard work and efforts, and may you reap the benefits of your hard work in this life and the Hereafter. Ameen.

This book is dedicated to all the parents of past and future
Essay Panel Contest participants who work
to please Allah (swt) by following His Teachings
and His Final Messenger, Muhammad (saw).

To mightier pens, sharper minds,
and in pursuit of a united, cohesive ummah.

"And that there is not for man except that [good]
for which he strives"
Al-Quran (Surah An-Najm 53:39)

"... And whoever desires the reward of this world –
We will give him thereof; and whoever desires the reward
of the Hereafter – We will give him thereof.
And we will reward the grateful."
Al-Quran (Surah Al-Imran 3:145)

Righteousness is not that you turn your faces toward the east
or the west, but [true] righteousness is [in] one who believes in
Allah, the Last Day, the angels, the Book, and the prophets and
gives wealth, in spite of love for it, to relatives, orphans, the needy,
the traveler, those who ask [for help], and for freeing slaves;
[and who] establishes prayer and gives zakah; [those who] fulfill
their promise when they promise; and [those who] are patient in
poverty and hardship and during battle. Those are the ones who
have been true, and it is those who are the righteous.
Al-Quran (Surah Al-Baqarah 2:177)

Nu'man Bin Bashir (ra) reported Allah's Messenger (saw)
as saying: "You see the believers as regards their being merciful
among themselves and showing love among themselves and being
kind, resembling one body, so that, if any part of the body is not
well then the whole body shares the sleeplessness (insomnia)
and fever with it."
Sahih Bukhari (Volume 8, Book 73, #40)

EPC Steering Committee:

Farid Ahmed, Ph.D.
Zahra B. Ahmed, M.D.
Mohammad S. Choudhury, Ph.D.
Mostafiz R. Chowdhury, Ph.D.
Ayman Nassar, M.Sc.
Mahfuz ur Rahman, M.Sc.

Editorial Committee:

Fatima Khan, Editor-in-Chief
Farid Ahmed, Ph.D.
Zahra Ahmed, M.D.
Mohammad S. Choudhury, Ph.D.
Zahirah Lynn Eppard
Mahfuz ur Rahman, M.Sc.

Graphic Design: Sakinah Productions
sakinah.productions@gmail.com

Foreword

It is convenient to say we aim to raise leaders. It is convenient to say we develop writing and oratory skills in our youth. It is convenient to say we teach children through opportunities such as essay and speech competitions. In a certain sense, we do. The truth is, however, that we are gardeners of an already planted bed of seeds. We do not "grow" the plants. We simply assist in giving the plants what they need so they can nourish and grow themselves.

One of the needs of children is platforms that provide healthy socialization, provide opportunities where they can learn and challenge themselves by trying something new, provide opportunities for reflection about themselves and the world around them.

By giving a platform where children can be heard today, we pray to be indebted to these children when they become future leaders, honest workers, fathers & mothers, artists, entrepreneurs, thinkers, writers, diplomats, doctors, lawyers, engineers, teachers, scientists, artisans, businessmen, and inventors. And above all we pray that we become beneficiaries of these precious gifts and lovers of God, Ameen.

Adib Ahmed
Graduate Student
George Washington University
Past Participant and Judge

Preface

All praise, the best of praise, belongs to Allah (swt) for giving us the means and method to present Volume 9 of the Young Muslim Voices publication. This volume includes three years of essays from our annual Essay Panel Contest (EPC). Muslim youth in and around the Washington, D.C. metropolitan area wrote their essay submissions on different themes each year. Participants at all age levels demonstrated a profound understanding of the topics and how they relate them to their personal and communal lives.

The following essays were written with great dedication and hard work. I hope that through this writing process, our youth internalized the meaning of morality and will help express their newfound understandings with our valued readers. May Allah accept our children's efforts, increase their thirst for knowledge, and help them spread their knowledge through eloquent writing and speech. May Allah also accept EPC's humble efforts to maintain this program and reward all of our volunteers and contributors in the Hereafter. Ameen.

Mohammad O. Mahboob
President
Mafiq Foundation, Inc.

A Reflection
on the Judging Process

I want to start by first acknowledging that it is a great honor to be a judge in the yearly EPC essay competition. Having judged three EPC events in prior years, this fourth event did not fail to impress with the quality of essays submitted by the students. Being the father of two busy teens overwhelmed with school work, Islamic studies, chores and life commitments, I know firsthand how difficult it is for students to find the time to work on the EPC essay, but fortunately so many participate and do a fantastic job! Thus, making judging of this competition an enjoyable activity from which the students and judges both benefit. Before I talk about the many benefits of this competition, a review of the process is needed so as to fully respect the hard work that goes into arranging an event of this magnitude.

Numerous essay topics are initially considered but eventually an essay topic is assigned that is most pertinent to societal issues being encountered by our youth such as bullying and racism, and for which our faith provides the answers. Thus, in writing the essay, the student not only must discuss the problems they face today but also must encompass the teachings of our prophet, lessons from our holy Quran, and wisdom from the hadiths and discuss how our faith emboldens them to overcome the adversity that challenges them.

Students are given several weeks to develop, write and submit their essays, after which the judging starts with the judges receiving seemingly an overwhelming number of essays. I personally read the essays several times before I assign grades and finally, this culminates with a hectic day full of eloquent speeches and other events. The speech portion of the essay contest is to allow the students a chance to verbally express their writing style that otherwise would be missed. It's a chance for them to shine! In addition, they are gaining valuable experience in public speaking which is a critical skill that I myself wish would have learned earlier in my life. Thus, the EPC essay and speech competition helps students by empowering them with the skills and confidence they need to become successful and productive members of the community.

As a judge, what amazes me is the courage of the children! Many have to overcome shyness of speaking in front of others while others overcome language barriers as their English skills might not be so fluent. No matter the situation, the dedication to write a quality essay and prepare a speech is commendable. Knowing this, I feel proud of our youth and am feel confident for the future of our community! Though this is a competition, every child who participates is a true winner because at the end, it's all about self-reflection on what actions can be taken to improve one's life and the lives of others. That is the goal of the EPC committee and the essay contest and that is the ultimate goal of our faith, indeed.

Dr. Kamran Anwar
EPC Judge

In the Name of Allah, The Most Gracious, The Most Merciful

Introduction

The 9th volume of the Young Muslim Voices (YMV) is a special one in that it is a compilation of three years of winning Essay Panel Competition essays. These winning essays were written through the hard work of young Muslims throughout the Washington D.C. area, and showcase diverse experiences and perspectives. The essays also provide us with an insight to the incredible capabilities of our future leaders, and share countless examples of the inspiring messages they have shared. We thank Allah (swt) for allowing us to be a part of the EPC community and allowing us the opportunity to see the Muslim youth use their imagination, intellect, and critical thinking to communicate their ideas beautifully through their writing.

While enjoying the growth of the Annual EPC competition, we must appreciate the community that has done so much for this project since 2002. Without the hard work of all our community members, judges, volunteers, participants, parents of participants, committee members, editorial staff, and sponsors, we could not have gotten where we are today and for that we thank you. May Allah (swt) accept the hard word of everyone involved as righteous deeds, Ameen. All efforts would be nothing without the help and blessing of Allah (swt), and Alhamdulillah, we are truly blessed.

EPC Program Structure

A brief outline of EPC's program structure is provided below for those who are not familiar with the process or those who may want to replicate the program in their own communities.

First, an overall theme is determined that relates to the everyday experiences of American Muslims in the current societal context. Essay contest topics are then selected to encourage the youth to examine and ponder different Islamic subjects encouraging them to increase their imaan, gain analytical skills, and practice their ability to express their beliefs and thoughts effectively through written communication.

Each year, students from elementary school to college compete in the theme-based essay contest. This edition of the YMV book has three years of essays, and therefore three different topics. In the first round of the competition, students write an essay based on specific guidelines for submission including theme, formatting, number of citations, etc. There are three development-based levels in the competition: elementary school, middle school, and high school/ college.

The elementary level focuses on basic application of the principles of Islam and its message. The middle school level requires a deeper understanding than the elementary level, and focuses on matters concerning morality and character. Finally, the high school level topics require reflection on and analysis on contemporary issues facing Muslim societies.

The competition starts with the essays being read, scored, and ranked by judges. The authors of the highest scoring essays from this first round are then moved to the second round where they participate in a speech competition. Finally, a collection of the winning essays is compiled and published in the YMV series. Moreover, EPC extends beyond the written and spoken essays, and includes multimedia and poster competitions. These two are creative components of the contest, and we've seen amazing examples of the participant's artistic and analytical skills. Some examples of these posters will be included throughout this book.

Throughout this book, the central theme of each annual contest will be presented followed by the specific prompts the students were given and the winning essays. We hope you enjoy reading these essays as much as we did, and that you are inspired by the participants' ability to analyze complex issues and communicate them in beautiful, well written essays.

Fatima Khan
Editor-in-Chief
Young Muslim Voices, Volume 9

2017

Faith Through Action

Essay Panel Contest

2017

This poster was submitted by Zakariya Qaadri in the Level 1 competition.

ELEMENTARY SCHOOL, LEVEL 1
Grades 1 & 2

Faith in Action

Write a letter to your beloved one telling him/her what the first three verses of Surah al-Ma'un mean to you and how you can practice them in your classroom or neighborhood.

FIRST PLACE
Mariyah Mehmood, Silver Spring, Md.
MCC Weekend School and Bushy Park Elementary School

Dear Nani,

How are you? Guess what? I learned something amazing. I learned surah Maun, it means small kindness.

There are 3 important lessons in this surah. Allah is describing a bad person in the first 3 ayahs.The first ayah is about a person who doesn't believe in the day of judgement. That is Yawmud-deen. The next ayah is about a person who doesn't take care and is not generous to the orphan (yateem). The third ayah says he doesn't feed the poor. But he also tells others not to feed the poor and needy miskeen.

I applied these lessons in my community, my neighborhood, and my classroom. I collected money to buy a toy. But I heard an old lady say that she needed a bus ticket. I gave all my money to her and she was very thankful. Also in my school a girl got bullied and was crying. I gave her one of my stickers and she hugged me.

As a Muslim, I should be kind to others. My mom started a group called Muslim Scouts of Maryland. We learn the value of community service. Every month we do activities like feeding the homeless in DC, preparing dental kits, and making blankets for sick kids. I hope Allah sees these small kindnesses. I want to be a good Muslim who makes people smile. I want Allah to smile at me.

Love,
Your granddaughter

References:
Surah al-Ma'un 107:1-3

SECOND PLACE
Yusuf Mehmood, Silver Spring, Md.
MCC Weekend School and Bushy Park Elementary School

Dear Abbu,

How are you? I love you! I learned a new surah called surah Al-Maun. It means small kindnesses. There are 3 cool points in this surah's first 3 ayahs. I learned that a bad person doesn't do 3 things:

1. He doesn't believe in the Day of Judgement (Yawm-ud-deen).
2. He doesn't take care of the orphan (Yateem).
3. And he doesn't feed the poor but he also tells other people not to feed the poor (miskeen).
    (Recite in Arabic)

I don't want to be a bad Muslim. I want to make sure I do good things. My mom came to my public school to teach the 1st graders about Islam. I confidently read surah Fatiha. Everyone was amazed and clapped. I am proud to be a muslim. My religion teaches me to be kind to others. In Muslim scouts of Maryland, I learned about how to help people. I made food packets for people who are needy. I went to a shelter house to give people the lunches. They were so happy to see me. At bedtime I ask my mom why do we believe in the Day of Judgement. She told me living in this world is like studying for a test. We do good things so on the Day of Judgement, we can see if we passed the test. If we get an 'A' we go to jannah. I don't want to get an 'F' because that means hell fire. So I try my best to be kind to people who are lonely at lunch and at recess. I also share my clothes and toys with people from Syria, they are so happy to get nice things. In shaa Allah I want to share my Eid money with them. I hope Allah is proud of me.

Love,
Your Grandson

References:
Surah al-Ma'un 107:1-3

THIRD PLACE
Hafsah Khan, College Park, Md.
Al Huda School

Assalam Alaikum Warahmatullahi Wabarakatuh

Dear Sakina,

How are you? My Islamic studies teacher taught us all about surah Ma'un and I wanted to share what I learned with you. Can you believe that some people think that the day of judgement isn't true! They are mean to the orphans! They don't even tell others to feed the poor! My teacher said feed the poor and be kind and generous to the orphans. We should help the Syrian families that moved to America. I will ask my parent if we can have a food drive and maybe we can meet the orphans and become friends with them and give them gifts. I know you like to bake treats so maybe you could have a bake sale to raise money for the poor. Let's make lots of dua for the hungry, poor, and the orphans.

Essay Panel Contest

2017

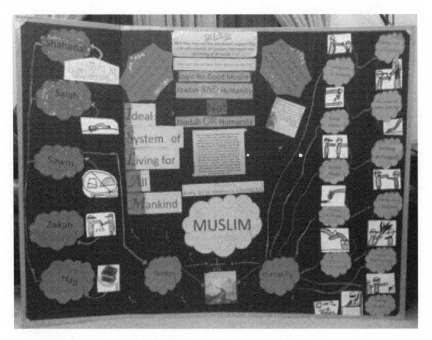

This poster was submitted by Ahmad Imam in the Level 2 competition.

Faith in Action

**Think about the first three verses of
Surah Ma'un. What can you do in your
neighborhood or in your classroom
in order to show the teachings
from these verses?
Think about the actions or good deeds
you can perform to spread the teachings
of Islam just as the early Muslims
were told to do.**

FIRST PLACE
Talha Jafri, Potomac, Md.
Travilah Elementary School

Sura Ma'un is an important Sura revealed in Mecca to show the bad behavior of some who do not believe (probably Abu-Sufyan, Walid-ibn-i-Muqayrah or 'As-ibn-i–Wa'il) in the Day of Judgement (1,2). The translation of Sura Ma'un1 says that the person who does not believe in the rewards and punishments in the Hereafter does not take care of the orphan or give to the needy. By this, Sura Ma'un1 tells us that we should feed the poor and care for the orphans (2). This is important not only because we get rewards, but that we are a big community and we should help everyone in the community.

The first line suggests that you should believe in the Hereafter and the punishments and reward that people get for how they behave. You get rewards for giving to the orphans and to the poor and Allah says that if you give charity it will get multiplied up to seven hundred times for you after you die.

The second line talks about orphans. To help the orphans, I can go to the orphanage and give them clothes, water, food, toys, and more. We can also give them support and make some clothing drives and toy drives and efforts to get them what they need. I go with my parents to charity event where they donate to the poor and orphans.

The third line says to feed the poor or needy. To feed the poor you can go to shelters and give them food and you can also help serve the meals. You can also organize a food drive for you school and in your community. Maybe to feed the poor you can donate to food drives everywhere to get food to lots of poor people in different places. My regular school, Islamic weekend school, and my soccer team all have food drives.

To get more people to donate, you can go to more people you know and ask them to donate and explain to them why it is good. I would tell them that some of the poor and orphans do not have food, clothes and toys. By donating you can get them shelter, food, clothes, clean water, and toys. They should care, because if they were one of the poor people, they would want people to help them. So they should help them. Also, you do not know if you will become one of the needy in the future. For example, your house might burn down, you could lose your job, and your parents could die. None of us know the future, only Allah.

I hope that you learned a lot about Sura Ma'un1 from my essay. I learned that what Sura Ma'un1 means while writing my essay. The Sura reminded me to be conscious of my deeds for the Hereafter and to take care of orphans and the poor. I also thought of how I can apply it to my life. I need to take action to help the orphans and the poor.

References:
1. Al-Quran Surah al-Ma'un 107:1-3
2. Surah al-Ma'un, Chapter 107. Al-Islam.org. Web. 14 Jan. 2017.

SECOND PLACE
Yusrah Baqqi-Barrett, Laurel, Md.
Baqqi Academy

It made me really sad to see a homeless person not get any of the food we brought to feed them. We had just run out of food when he arrived to the park where we were serving it last fall, and he became really upset. I could tell he was worried about when he would be able to eat again and I knew he would not get any food for a while. In the Qur'an, Allah tells us to not be like the person who does not feed the poor or take care of orphans. Helping to feed the homeless has helped me see why it is important for Muslims to show their faith through doing good deeds. There are many ways I can put my faith into action and help the people who need it.

One way I am planning to put my faith into action is by making blankets for the homeless people of Baltimore for my Girl Scout service project later this month. I chose to make blankets because feeding people is not the only way we can take care of others. People who are homeless don't have many places they can stay during the winter and many will need the blankets because they will have to sleep outside in the cold. I have helped collect blankets before, but by making them, I get to pick out fun colors and patterns. I really enjoyed making blankets before in my art class, and realized I could use what I learned to make more for the homeless.

Another way I can show what Islam teaches is by feeding the homeless. I want to help by donating food as much as I can. I have been to Baltimore City a few times to serve hot food and hand out lunches to the homeless that they could take with them for when they got hungry again. I would like to go back and serve food to them as often as possible to help stop them from going hungry, even if it is just for a little while.

Finally, we should also remember orphans who have lost their parents and not just the homeless. A way to help take care of both the homeless and the orphans is by asking other people to donate money. There are charities like Islamic Relief that collect money for orphans and give it to their guardians for anything they might need. The money goes to pay for things like their school and doctor visits (2). Donating money to the homeless can help because then they can choose their own food and they can have enough money to buy the food they like. I learned from collecting food donations for a shelter in Baltimore that sometimes when people donate food, they only think to give a lot of the same types of things. People that need food can get tired of eating these things and eating the same foods may not give them all the nutrition they need to be healthy.

Allowing people to choose what they want to eat is also a way to be nice to them.

There are many ways that I can help people who need it the most. Making blankets to keep people warm, feeding people who are hungry, and asking people to donate money to help others get what they need are all ways I can do this. By doing good deeds and helping others, I can show that I believe in Islam and put my faith into action.

References:
1. Al-Quran Surah al-Ma'un 107:1-3
2. Islamic Relief, Orphan Sponorship. Retrieved from http://www.islamic-relief.org/faq/orphan-sponsorship/

THIRD PLACE
Shabbir Khan, Baltimore, Md.
Al-Rahmah School

In surah al Maun Allah told us to practice his commands and our faith:

> "Have you seen him who denies the Requital? (1) So, he is the one who pushes away the orphan (2) And he does not persuade others to feed the poor (3)."

It is important to realize that the faith we do have, we should try to practice in our lives. We should share all the blessings that Allah had granted us with those who do not have enough money to make a living.

I try my best to practice Allah's commands by giving my clothes whenever there is a clothes drive. I donate money for the orphan drive from the savings that I have in my rocket ship bank. I try to save some money from my lunch and bake sale allowance I get from my parents and give that to the orphan drive.

We should all try to practice this and try to look around us if we have someone in our school or neighborhood who needs help.

Allah and the prophets kept on emphasizing these things. One example is in Surah al Fajr: "No! But you do not honor the orphan (17) and you do not encourage one another to feed the needy (18)."

We should not only try to help them with money and other things but also give them respect and should not let them down by any of our behavior. By acting upon all those commands of Allah, we actually thank Him for all His blessings on us. The best part is, we will be able to earn His love and his rewards in both dunya and aakhirah.

Essay Panel Contest
2017

This poster was submitted by Ali Serif in the Level 3 competition.

Faith in Action

**In the light of Surah Balad (verses 13-18) and Surah Fajr (verses 17-20) – think about how early Muslims were commanded to serve the community and perform selfless good deeds, like feeding the hungry, helping the needy, and taking care of the orphans in their neighborhood.
What can you do in your school, neighborhood, and the community at large to exemplify these values and how can you prepare yourself for the values discussed in the Surahs?**

FIRST PLACE
Rafia Zafar, Baltimore, Md.
Al-Rahmah School

The Good Deed

Schools, neighborhoods, and communities can perform good deeds by doing things such as helping and donating to the poor and taking care of the orphans around us. By doing things as little as these, we can help our community and perform good deeds to help our community.

In Surah-al-Balad (verses 13-18) Allah talks about the people who give food to the poor and who help the orphans, the people on the Right Hand. In Surah-al-Fajr (verses 17-20) Allah talks about the people who don't feed the poor and he says that those people are greedy and they keep their wealth to themselves.

To exemplify these values, we can donate clothes and blankets to the poor and we can take care of the orphans by giving them food and clothes. In Surah-al-Balad, Allah says "Or giving in a day of hunger." This can encourage us to feed the poor and the needy.

We all know that donating and helping the needy leads us to Allah's Path, but we are still greedy and selfish. We don't pay so much attention to who needs more money, we just care about ourselves. In the Quran, Allah says, "And spend of that wherewith we have provided you time before death cometh unto one of you and he said: My Lord! If only you would reprieve me for a little while, then I would have given money and be among the righteous." (63:10)

The Prophet said: "The believer's shade on the Day of Judgment will be his charity." (Al-Tirmidhi) On the Day of Judgment there will be no shade but Allah will shade the people who gave charity and helped the poor. If we give charity and help the poor, we will be protected by Allah on the Day of Judgment, In shaa Allah.

If we can take some time and do these simple things, we can serve our community, perform good deeds to help our community, and help ourselves on the Day of Judgment.

References:
1. Zakat Foundation of America "Why is Charity so Important" Nov 10 2014,
http://www.zakat.org/blog/why-is-charity-so-important-in-islam/
Accessed January 14, 2017
2. Sound Vision "Quran and Ahadeeth on the poor and the needy"
http://www.soundvision.com/article/quran-and-ahadith-on-the-poor-and-needy
Accessed January 14, 2017
3. Quran Explorer -
http://read.quranexplorer.com/63/10/10/Usmani/Mishari-Rashid/Eng-Pickthal-Audio/Tajweed-OFF (Surah 63:Ayaha 10)
Accessed on January 14, 2017

SECOND PLACE
Areeb Gani, Silver Spring, Md.
Takoma Park Middle School

Surah Balad was revealed in Mecca when the disbelievers were opposing the Prophet Muhammad (saw – Peace be upon him) through various means. Surah Fajr is another Meccan surah that was revealed when disbelievers of Mecca started to show hostility to the new Muslims and started to persecute them. In ayahs 13-18 in Surah Balad, Allah says that those who free slaves, give necessities on days of critical needs or famine, donate to orphans and donate to the needy will be among the believers and will be companions of the Right Hand. In ayahs 17-20 of Surah Fajr, Allah compares the men who do not honor the orphans and encourage one another to feed the poor to the people of 'Ad, Thamud and Iram, inhabitants of prior civilization who were punished for their disobedience to Allah. Allah also talks about the characteristics of the people who are arrogant when they receive wealth, and boastfully say, "Allah has honored me.", but when they are tested through hardship on their wealth they say in despair that, "Allah has humiliated me."

What we learn from these ayahs is that Allah is calling the believers to action; he is calling the believer to work for social welfare. Specifically, he is calling the believers to help and encourage others to help those who are poor, orphans, and slaves. In Surah Fajr, Allah says that those who work for the welfare of the people are among the believers and among the companions of the Right Hand. This means that those who are involved in addressing the need for the others will be protected by Allah and receive His blessings.

In order for me to be counted as a believer and to receive the special status of being placed under the Right Hand of Allah, I can take some specific actions. For example, the first thing I can start working on is making everyone aware of Allah's commandments for social welfare. I can start with my family, and then spread the message to others in my community. I can then work with others to take actions to address the needs poor and orphans in our society. One of the ways to do this is by leading and participating in different kinds of drives such as food drives where I can collect and distribute dry and canned foods to the needy and poor people within my community. During the winter months, I can collect and distribute warm clothes to those who are in need for these items and are unable to buy them. I can also organize volunteers in my local masjid to visit the local homeless shelter and help distribute foods. During the time of Eid Ul Adha, I can work with my local masjid and my community to collect the meats from their sacrifices and help distribute that to the poor within the community.

I could also contribute to the charities through monthly donations for the orphans and try to encourage others to do the same. These small donations can help the orphans to become educated and avoid child labor which is similar to slavery during the Meccan period. During the month of Ramadan I can work with others to organize Iftar and help distribute meals to those who can't afford it. I can also help collect Zakat al Fitr and buy clothes and foods for the needy and help distribute those prior to the Eid so that they can also celebrate this wonderful holiday.

In my school, I can share the message of helping the needy to everyone, since these are not only values taught in the Quran, but also universal values. Therefore I can get non-muslims in my school involved as well. I can then work with the students in my school to raise funds through bake sale, t-shirt sale or by other means and send the money to third world countries to help the children there who are unable to go to school, unable to get access to safe drinking water, forced to do labor, and do not have a proper place to live.

I could also write articles in local newspapers and talk to representatives or congressmen about the importance of taking care of the needy within our community and urge them to help these people.

As I grow older, I can participate in charities and clubs such as Muslim Students Association and work with others to initiate community service projects such as donating food, money, and helping rebuild homes, shelter and schools.

THIRD PLACE
Deemah Abusway, Baltimore, Md.
Al-Rahmah School

Allah says in Surah Al-Balad ayat 13-20, it's the freeing of a slave, or feeding on a day of severe hunger, an orphan of near relationship, or a needy person in misery, and then being among those who believed and advised one another to patience and advised one another to compassion, those are the companions of the right, but they who disbelieved in Our signs-those are the companions of the left, over them will be fire closed in. In this surah Allah tells us about the companions of the left and right. He tells us what will happen to them.

Mankind was commanded to do good deeds by Allah very early in time. Not everyone wanted to. For some people it was what they didn't do that got them farther and farther away from their deen which means their faith weakened. If you keep doing good deeds, In shaa Allah you will be a companion of the right.

Good deeds don't have to be anything major. Start in your house. You can do chores without being asked and listen to your parents. Take care of your siblings so your parents don't get a headache. Stay out of trouble and do your homework.

You can move up a notch and get more good deeds by helping in your neighborhood. Pick up trash and also recycle. Help your neighbors wash their cars or bake or cook something for them. Help clean tables and collect balls and jump ropes after lunch and recess.

You can help out at your community by visiting a homeless shelter and volunteer to pass out food, clothes, or blankets to them. Donate money to help people in need. You should visit an orphanage and spread some love and volunteer there as well. Give homeless people and orphans Quran lessons and give them education if needed. You could donate money and clothes to mosques and they can distribute them to those in need.

All of these actions show how strong your faith is. If you have strong in Allah you'll do these for sure and be a good Muslim because you know Allah will In shaa Allah grant us Jannah in the hereafter. So gather all these good deeds and be the best Muslim you can be.

References:
1. Tarhuni, Omar. "The Good Deeds."
www.khutbahbank.org.uk/Royal_Holloway_khutbahs/Omar_
Tarhuni/good_deeds.h
2. https://quran.com

Essay Panel Contest

2017

This poster was submitted by Jannah Nassar in the Level 4 competition.

Faith in Action

**In the light of Surah Balad (verses 13-18) and Surah Fajr (verses 17-20) – think about how early Muslims were commanded to serve the community and perform selfless good deeds, like feeding the hungry, helping the needy, and taking care of the orphans in their neighborhood.
What can you do in your school, neighborhood, and the community at large to exemplify these values and how can you prepare yourself for the values discussed in the Surahs?**

FIRST PLACE
Ramlah Amsa, College Park, Md.
Al Huda School

In Surah Balad ayahs 13-18, Allah (swt) highlights the importance of helping those in need, feeding the poor, and taking care of orphans. In Surah Fajr ayahs 17-20, Allah talks about those who don't perform these good deeds. During the Prophet's (saw) time, the early Muslims were commanded to do these things. They did them selflessly, just to please Allah (swt). For example, even though Shuayb Ar-Rumi (ra) was poor himself, he helped the other people who were poor, which is a reason that Umar (ra) admired him. Abdur-Rahman ibn Awf' (ra) was a very wealthy man who didn't let his wealth distract him from following the straight path. Just like these Sahabah, Muslims today should try to make dua and integrate these acts into their everyday lives, persuade others to be faithful and compassionate, and feed and take care of the needy and orphans.

There are many ways in which I could feed and care for the needy and orphans. "And give the relative his right, and (also) the poor and the traveler, and do not spend wastefully. Indeed, the wasteful are brothers of the devils, and ever has Shaytan been to his Lord ungrateful." (Al-Quran, Surah 17:26-27).One way is by funding enough money from a yard sale, bake sale, or lemonade stand to buy them new supplies that they may need to prosper in their life. Another way is by starting multiple collection drives in different parts of my community to muster uneaten foods and unused clothing to provide to the needy and orphans. Third, I could educate them so that they attain knowledge, leading them to getting a job and being successful in life. However, in order to do all this, I would need to have other people on my side helping us with this cause to save the needy and orphans.

In order to get other people on my side to help me with this cause, I need to first persuade them to be faithful and compassionate. I could do this by educating them, to let them know of this serious matter that we must deal with. I could start workshops, organize different functions, and do more that teaches them about this topic. Once they fully understand the seriousness of this matter, they might stand by my side to help save those in need of our help. Abu Qatadah said that the Prophet (saw) said, "If anyone would like Allah to save him from the hardships of the Day of Resurrection, he should give more time to his debtor who is short of money, or remit his debt altogether." (Muslim)

Also, I could make dua for the needy and orphans, praying that their future is better than their present life, and encourage my peers to do the same.

We shouldn't be like the people mentioned in Surah Fajr ayahs 17-20, but like the people in Surah Balad ayahs 13-18. We should cooperate and collaborate to help and care for the poor and orphans. We should educate ourselves so that we may teach them new things. Also, we should raise money and donate it to them to relieve them of their sufferings and hardships. As the Muslims from the Prophet's (saw) time did these things, why can't we do the same?

References:
1. Ahmad, A. (2014, August 27th). Top 10 Ways to Help Poor and Needy People. Linked In.
Retrieved from https://www.linkedin.com/pulse/201408272147
10-141895933-top-10-ways-to-help-poor-and-needy-people
2. Editorial. (2009, April 30th). The Sahaba's sacrifice in the path of Allah. TheKhalifah. Retrieved from http://www.khilafah.com/
the-sahabas-sacrifice-in-the-path-of-allah/
3. Mujahid, A.M. (n.d.). Quran and Ahadith on the poor and needy. Sound Vision. Retrieved from http://www.soundvision.
com/article/quran-and-a-hadith-on-the-poor-and-needy

SECOND PLACE
Musa Ahmad, Lanham, Md.
Homeschool

Albert Einstein once said, "The high destiny of the individual is to serve rather than to rule." Watching the news every day and witnessing the countless problems in my local and global community saddens me. As a young American Muslim what can I do to serve my community and resolve these issues? The solution is three dimensional, or 3D: Dawah, Donations, and Du'a.

When we hear the word Da'wah, the first thing that probably comes to our minds is telling others about Islam. However, in this case, Da'wah means more than that. It means spreading awareness of the issues people are facing and encouraging them to take action, as Allah says in Surah Balad, "And then being among those who believed and advised one another to patience and advised one another to compassion." (Al-Quran, 90:17). Many Americans have no idea about problems such as hunger, orphan hood, and poverty, and are overtaken by greed, so we need to give them Da'wah so they are not counted among the people about whom Allah says in Surah Fajr, "No! But you do not honor the orphan, and you do not encourage one another to feed the poor, and you consume inheritance, devouring (it) altogether, and you love wealth with immense love." (Al-Quran, 89:17-20). Da'wah is not just about advising non-Muslims, but also advising Muslims, who have a greater responsibility.

Another way to serve our community is through donating. Donating does not only include donating money, but we can also donate our time and capabilities. If you are young like me, even walking around at a fundraising dinner holding a donation box or volunteering at a hospital could be considered donating time and capability, and could earn you Jannah. Donating can be difficult but it pays off, as Allah says in Surah Balad, "And what can make you know what is (breaking through) the difficult pass. It is the freeing of a slave, or feeding on a day of severe hunger, an orphan of near relationship or a needy person in misery." (Al-Quran, 90:11-16). If we do this, we will become people of faith, patience, and compassion. Allah then mentions their reward when He says, "Those are the companions of the right." (Al-Quran, 90:18). Being companions of the right is a great honor because it means that on the Day of Judgement we will receive our book of deeds in our right hand. We, as Muslims, have to donate according to our capabilities, whether it is something big like freeing a slave or even something small like volunteering at a local homeless shelter. If a man who has three million dollars donates one million, and a little girl who has three dollars donates one, the little girl could earn more reward than the man depending on their intentions and capabilities, so never belittle any donation, because every penny counts!

We may think that giving Da'wah and donating are the most important solutions, but actually the most effective solution is Du'a. The prophet (saw) said "Nothing can change divine decree except Du'a." (Ibn Majah, Book #36, Hadith #97). We should make Du'a for the success of our communities and for Allah to ease the suffering of people all over the world. Allah guarantees His servants that He will answer their prayers, as He says in Surah Baqarah, "And when my servant asks you, (O Muhammad), concerning me – indeed I am near. I respond to the invocation of the supplicant when he calls upon me. So let them respond to (by obedience) and believe in me that they may be (rightly) guided." (Al-Quran, 2:186). As Muslims, we need to make it a routine every day to make plenty of Du'a, because not everyone can do Da'wah or donate, but everyone, no matter who or where they are, can make Du'a.

In conclusion, as American Muslims, we can serve our communities through Da'wah, donating, and Du'a. We have to give as much effort as we can, because Allah will not ask us about the results, but He will ask us what effort we made to make the world a better place. We should remember that everything Allah does to us, good or bad, is a test, and to pass it, we need to serve our community. We have to make people aware, and encourage them to show mercy, kindness, and compassion to others, and to avoid greed. We need to give as much money and time as we can afford to, and we need to raise our hands, day and night, to Allah in Du'a. May Allah make us among the companions of the right and make us among those who encourage patience and compassion. Ameen.

References:
1. https://www.brainyquote.com/quotes/quotes/a/alberteins165190.html
2. Quran, Sahih International Translation (https://sunnah.com/ibnmajah/36/97)

THIRD PLACE
Erfan Hamza, College Park, Md.
Al Huda School

What is a Muslims identity? Identity of a Muslim is a person with perfect character. Muslims are God fearing, honest, decent, kind, peaceful, and free of immorality. For a Muslim, character is very important. Prophet Muhammad (saw) said "I only have been sent to perfect the character". The word "Muslim" means one who submits to the will of God. Allah says in the holy Quran "Allah is with you wherever you may be, and Allah sees all what you do" (Al-Quran, 57:4). Therefore, we must maintain our identity in real and virtual world or online as well.

Internet is being misused today by evil people. It became a tool for cybercrime. False propaganda, cyber bully, hate crime, identity theft, indecency is so obvious today through Internet. Allah says in the holy Quran "I have created the jinn and humankind only for My worship" (Al-Quran, 51:56). As a Muslim anything we do, we must verify whether our action is pleasing or displeasing Allah. It could be in public, private or online. One main concern is cyber bullying. Social media, websites or blogs are being used to bully people. Character assassination is very common in the Internet.

Bullying is strictly prohibited by the Quran and Sunnah because Allah says: O ye who believe, let not some men among you laugh at others, it may be that the latter are better than the former, nor defame nor be sarcastic to each other nor call each other offensive nicknames, ill seeing is a name connoting wickedness to be used of one after he has believed, and those who do not desist are indeed doing wrong (Al-Quran, 49:11). Bullying can cause depression and lead people to hate themselves. And that is definitely not of the character of a Muslim. And Allah will definitely punish a person who ridicules or bullies others. Muslims believe in accountability of every action and every word we utter. Allah says in the holy Quran "So, by your Lord (O Muhammad), We shall certainly call all of them to account for everything they used to do" (Al-Quran, 15:92-93). A Muslim also believes that everything that we say and do is recorded. Allah says in the holy Quran "Not a word does he (or she) utter, but there is a watcher by him ready (to record it)" (Al-Quran, 50:18). Therefore, a Muslim must remember his or her faith when goes online. The purpose of the internet is to help people and make things easier. Social media such as Facebook can be used to share the difficult condition of people in many countries with the world. Global awareness can be raised via social media. At the same time, we can use social media for bad reasons such as to hurt someone or spread false propaganda. If we remember that Allah is always watching us and we are created to worship only Him, it can help us to overcome our desires and please Allah. Another common thing on the internet is spreading rumors. Spreading rumors is displeasing to Allah and it affects the character of a Muslim. So we should avoid spreading rumors because Allah says "when you rumored it with your tongues, and spoke with your mouths what you had no knowledge of, and you considered it trivial, but according to God, it is serious" (Al-Quran, 24:15). Sadly, many people do so; we should encourage people to stop spreading rumors and hurting people. We must verify any information comes to us from Internet and other sources. Allah says in the holy Quran "O you, who believe, if a disobedient person comes to you with news, verify it, lest you harm people in ignorance, and afterwards you become regretful to what you have done" (Al-Quran, 46:6). Another common thing that people do on the internet is spying and gossiping. That is not of a Muslim's character. Allah says: O ye who believe, avoid suspicion as much as possible, for suspicion in some cases is sin, and spy not on each other nor speak ill of each other behind their backs, would any of you like to eat the flesh of your dead brother, nay ye would abhor it but fear Allah for Allah is oft returning (Al-Quran, 49:11). The reason why people spy is to steal information or get into other's business. A Muslim should allow people to maintain their privacy. Internet is an open field of immorality, filled with tons of inappropriate and indecent websites. A Muslim cannot indulge with immorality. Allah says: those who love to see immorality spread among the believers, for them is a painful punishment, in this life and in the hereafter, God knows, and you do not know (Al-Quran, 24:15). Allah also says: O you, who believe, do not follow Satan's footsteps, whoever follows his footsteps he advocates obscenity and immorality, were it not for God's grace towards you, and his mercy, not one of you would have been pure, ever. But God purifies whomever he wills; God is all hearing, all knowing (Al-Quran, 24:21). So we should strive to perfect our character and avoid immorality. By maintaining our Muslim identity online we could show people the novel character of Muslim. If we succeed in doing so, people would follow us and we wouldn't be in the situation we are in today. We won't be considered terrorists and will be loved and followed by people.

One of the good attributes and values of human beings is the possibility of being caliph or representative of Allah on His earth. This is the highest value or perfection that one may reach. Allah says in the holy Quran "I will create a vicegerent on earth" (Al-Quran, 2:30). We must respect this honor and fulfill our role given by our Lord by establishing peace and justice in real and virtual world. Only it could be possible when we maintain our Muslim identity without compromising at anywhere for any cost.

Essay Panel Contest

2017

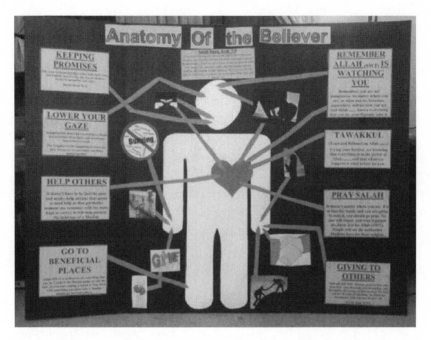

This poster was submitted by Danyah Imam in the Level 5 competition.

HIGH SCHOOL, LEVEL 5
Grades 9 & 10

Faith in Action

Consider how the early Muslims and today's faith-based communities overcame their contemporary social challenges; write an essay to identify the services/actions Musliums in America can undertake to address the social challenges of today. Use Surah Ihsan (verses 7-9) as your guide.

Please provide historical examples and practical strategies/actions to address the issues under current socio-political context.

FIRST PLACE
Danyah Imam, Catonsville, Md.
Western School of Technology and Environmental Science

From the start of Islam, Muslims have always faced social challenges, no matter when or where they were from. Many of these trials were the same as those that American Muslims face today, a prominent example being political resentment for Islam and its followers. However, it was instigated by different people in different times. In the Prophet (saw)'s time, this social confrontation came from the Quraysh, whereas in these days in America, the struggle is instigated by the media and the politics of today. However different or similar these challenges are, there is also a constant that is present in every time period: the religion of Islam, and the guidelines that come with it. Muslims with their Tawakkul, actions, and words can address the social challenges present in America today.

During the time of Rasulullah (saw) Muslims had to face countless trials, many of them stemming from the hatred they faced from their community, family, and friends. Rasulullah (saw) himself had been persecuted for spreading the message of Islam. Muslims in America today also face persecution from the non-Muslim community, some even facing it from their families and friends. However, throughout the trials that the Muslims faced in the past, Tawakkul, or their trust and reliance on Allah (swt), helped them face their social challenges. When the Muslims were boycotted by the Quraysh, when they were stopped from performing 'Umrah the year the Treaty of Hudaibiyah was signed, and on many other occasions, it was Tawakkul in Allah (swt) and their trust in Rasulullah (saw) that led them to accept whatever inevitably happened. They tried their hardest to accomplish their goals, but their strong faith and trust in Allah (saw) was what mattered in the end. They knew that whatever happened would be part of Allah (swt)'s plan for them, and the people around them. Similarly,

Muslims in America today should try their hardest to address their challenges in the best way they can, but in the end, Allah (swt) is the one who knows what will happen, and what is best. After all, it is in Surah Fatihah, which is recited in every Salah multiple times, that has the ayah which translates to, "You alone we worship, and you alone we ask for help." (Al-Quran, 1:5)

There are many physical actions can be taken to address the trials that American Muslims face today. After all, as Islam is the way of life, it also shows how Muslims are supposed to act, not only how to worship Allah (swt). The Sunnah of Rasulullah (saw) is mostly what is referred to when concerning how a Muslim should act, but the Qur'an also guides us about actions that should be undertaken as a believer. In Surah Insan, Allah (swt) says: "[The truly virtuous are] they [who] fulfil their vows, and stand in awe of a Day the woe of which is bound to spread far and wide, (7) and who give food - however great be their own want of it - unto the needy, and the orphan, and the captive, (8) [saying, in their hearts,] 'We feed you for the sake of God alone: we desire no recompense from you, nor thanks' (9)" (Al-Quran, Surah Insan 76:7-9).

This ayah mentions a few of the actions Muslims should take. When it talks about fulfilling vows, it implies that Muslims should always be trustworthy, even if it is just about keeping their word. Also, Muslims should give from their food to the poor and needy "...however great be their want of it..." This part of the Ayah is especially important, because it tells the Muslims to be selfless. It doesn't ask for Muslims to eat their fill and then offer the leftover food to the people in need, rather, it asks for those who can give food to think about others before they think about themselves, without hoping for anything in return (from them). These were two of the services and actions that the Muslim Ummah is encouraged to take when trying to address the social challenges of today. Not only will it display how Muslims act, but it also shows the character and morals that all Muslims should have.

The way a Muslim speaks to others goes alongside how he/she is supposed to act when addressing people who instigate the social challenges. Rasulullah (saw) was the greatest example of how people should address others who determinedly try to sully the message. Rasulullah (saw) was always patient, and remained calm, even when someone came and insulted him to his face. This is a great contrast from what some people do today. Whenever there is any misrepresentation of Islam in the media, some Muslims retaliate very harshly in a way that does not help get the true message of Islam across. The answer is not to ignore the misinformation, rather, it is to deal with it calmly, and to say things that will help rather than hurt the message that has to be conveyed.

Muslims in America have to deal with many social challenges today that are both very similar and rather different to the times of the early Muslims. However, even though there are slight differences in the trials that we have to face, it is the same guidelines that help us address them. Muslims must always have Tawakkul in Allah (swt), but they must do their best to address the issues alongside it. If the Muslim Ummah unites and carries out the instructions that Allah (swt) said to follow, then there will be no basis for other people, whether it be in America or anywhere else, to sully the name of Islam. It will not only create a sense of unity for Muslims themselves, but instead of causing further problems with the people determined to spread the hatred of Islam and Muslims, it will help draw them to the beauty of Islam.

References
1. "Quran Search." IslamiCity. N.p., n.d. Web. 15 Jan. 2017.
2. "Never Fear The Enemies Of Islam - Nouman Ali Khan||2017 - Awesome Lecture!" YouTube. YouTube, 07 Jan. 2017. Web. 15 Jan. 2017.
3. "The Quranic Arabic Corpus - Word by Word Grammar, Syntax and Morphology of the Holy Quran." The Quranic Arabic Corpus - Word by Word Grammar, Syntax and Morphology of the Holy Quran. N.p., n.d. Web. 15 Jan. 2017.

4. Shafi', Mufti Muhammad. Ma'ariful Qur'an. Ed. Muhammad Taqi 'Usmani. Vol. 8. Karachi: Maktaba-e-Darul-'Uloom, 2011. Print.

5. "Video Lectures." Nouman Ali Khan Collection. N.p., n.d. Web. 15 Jan. 2017.

SECOND PLACE
Amal Hossain, Hyattsville, Md.
College Park Academy

Have you ever been hungry? Like, I mean really hungry. Like, you haven't eaten the whole day kind of hungry. Well, I'm in a room full of muslims, so I'm sure everyone has been through a day of fasting. Anyone excited for Ramadan btw, it's only 131 days away, give or take a day or two. Anyways, Hunger. Let me tell you about an instance where a family was hungry. Like, they fasted for a day and only got to break their fast with water. On the second day, they only broke their fast with water. Afterwards, on the third day, they also only had water to break their fast. The most amazing part about that story is the fact that they had food on each of those days. However, they gave it away to a indigent, an orphan, and a captive who were begging for food. This is the story of none other than Ali (ra) and his family. Surah Insan verses 7 to 9 are based on this premise. The actions of this family were astoundingly selfless oppositions to social problems. Social challenges remain some of the most harrowing aspects of our time. Poverty, hatred and apathy plague our world, and are instrumental to the challenges which communities face today. Only by emulating the prophet pbuh and practicing generosity and sympathy can we solve these problems.

Money makes the world go round. Money is also the source of all evil. Regardless of what many people think, businesses, the economy, and wealth in general are crucial to our governments. However, they also cause innumerable unethical situations. One prominent element of money's destruction, is the distinct lack of it for many people. Lack of healthcare and medicine can cause death, but such amenities cost large amounts of money. 44 million people don't have health insurance, and are unable to pay for treatment of their illnesses. Poverty can also cause the death of 21,000 people, every day due to hunger. The response to this problem should be simple: feed the people and donate.. Lucky for us, Islam has a built in system to combat such struggles: Zakah and Sadaqah. Giving money to the impoverished can actually eliminate the lower class. Now you may be thinking that sounds impossible, however there are records of the Umayyad caliphate giving out so much zakah money that they eventually ran out of people to give it to. While the situations and circumstances may have been different, the concept of giving money to those less fortunate is still the same. The answer to poverty and hunger is simple; carrying it out is not. We need to be able to solve this problem by instilling the concept of giving selflessly. Give away in Allah's cause and your wealth will not decrease, but how many of us actually wholeheartedly believe that. It is also possible to combat hunger by organizing large scale soup kitchen and food drive efforts. If the entire muslim community was dedicating a sizeable portion of their time towards feeding those who were not well off, than they would be able to make sure that everyone ate a sizeable portion of food.

Another problem which our society faces today is hatred. There are unspoken amounts of hatred and general disgust towards different groups of people which are not present in the muslim community. This anger is deeply rooted in generalizations. A specific example is the Shia and sunni conflict which is taking place overseas. The amount of unwarranted hate which a person exudes upon seeing someone based sheerly on their beliefs is immense. There is a stigma in the muslim community that certain groups of people are better than others and some deserve less amiability than others. However, in Surah Mumtahina, verse 8, it is said that unless a person is evicting you unjustly from your residence, or fighting you over your deen, a muslim can show the same amount of geniality which they show their parents to outsiders. Take a moment to think about all the groups of people which you hate or were taught to hate. Can you honestly say they all fall in those categories? Even in surah Insan, ayah eight states that the righteous person is one who donates food to a prisoner of war. Actions such as donating food or showing care for people who are conventionally not respected is a huge catalyst for dismantling hatred. It's very important for muslims to realize that a large part of Islamophobia can be diffused by simply showing hospitality to our neighbors. However, we can't forget another crucial point; hatred exists against others, but outside of our communities. An example of this is the racism which exists towards minority groups. A specific race which is oppressed may not exist in our exact communities, however it is critical that we work to defend them as well. When it comes to stopping hatred it's not only what we look at, it's also what we're not looking at.

There are many social challenges which we can find around our communities. It's impossible to flawlessly solve them all and live in a utopian world, but it would be criminal not to try. The premises which ayah 8 in surah Insan give us are monumental. Being able to find the drive to selflessly help those who are less fortunate than ourselves is the basis of fixing an entire society. Perhaps that's the most beautiful part about generosity. If enough people are capable of opening up their hearts, then the effect reaches much wider than their own communities and people from all over will join in on the effort. The hatred which we can see within the muslim community and towards the muslim community is due to the stereotypes which are perpetuated by many ignorant people. We can overcome such hatred by making a new characteristic so prevalent that it will be the new face of muslim communities everywhere. That characteristic needs to be hospitality, kindness, and generosity.

References:
1. http://www.qtafsir.com/
2. https://ia800803.us.archive.org/26/items/
TheIslamicConquestOfSyria/Futuhusham_-_The_Islamic_
Conquest_of_Syria_-_Al_Waqidi.pdf

THIRD PLACE
Maryum Nassar, Clarksville, Md.
River Hill High School

Have you been looking at the news lately, and seeing what people think of us Muslims. These past few months have been very hard on us Muslims because of what we see on social media and what we experience in our everyday lives. We should not just accept the racist remarks people say to our faces, we should be stopping them. Trump has started many unacceptable lies and stereotypes about Muslims that aren't true. I believe we can change how people see Muslims and allow our communities to see the best in us. Today I am here to talk about what actions we can take to prevent certain situations from happening throughout our social lives. Muslim girls should not be looked upon differently just when entering a supermarket, they are normal people too. They should not fear going to school and getting comments like, "are you going to blow up the place" or "do you have a bomb in your scarf". Just because some Muslims may do this, it does not mean all do. In fact, in many places around where I live there are not any "bad" Muslims trying to hurt people. Society has labeled Muslims as terrorists and has not given us a chance to speak up. Things like "being a terrorist" really have an impact in our lives because once people hear this, they interpret us differently. People do not see the real part of us, the part of us that always gives sadaqa, feeds the hungry, helps the homeless, and performs selfless good deeds. We can change all of this, we can create a plan. My plan is to come together with other religious organizations like other masjids or churches. Collaborating with many different kinds of religions will allow people to see we are open minded and generous.

In surah Al-Insan ayah eight it says, "And they give food in spite of love for it to the needy, the orphan, and the captive". People need to see that Muslims aren't bad people and we do many good things, but society does not see that part of us. We can change this by giving out flyers to people we see around the streets. These flyers could explain Islam and could have a date that people would be able to come and ask questions. It is a person's choice to come or not but at least we are making an action. Another example is that we could have a Muslim funfest. Here children would be able to have fun while learning about Islam at the same time. Fun Fests draw many children to them, so they could bring lots of people. Not only do we need to inform non-muslims about Islam, but we need to inform the Muslim kids because they are setting the example of Muslims to other kids. Many kids these days are very judgmental and so seeing a young girl wearing a hijab will have an effect of what they think she is. Just because a child wears a hijab it does not mean they are not normal, they are every bit normal as anyone else.

Depending on where you live, if a child goes to a public school they could possibly be one of the only Muslims at the school. Therefore, they seem like they stand out and that's how others see them. I used to think in my school I was one of the only Muslims, but I was wrong. It turns out there are many more Muslims in my school that I didn't even know about. The reason I did not know was because we were all in different grades and did not talk to one another. In my school we have a MSA club. It stands for Muslim student association; this is a great way to get people involved in Islam. Not only did I meet new people in that club, but non-Muslims are invited to learn more about Islam too. So having an MSA at your schools will help people see what Islam is about. Another way to spread Islam and try to educate people on what is really right is by making videos about it. People are more likely to watch videos than read something because it seems more entertaining. By creating a video or short film we could be educating our communities on what we believe is right. The short film could be on anything informative about Islam or even about collaborating with other organizations. Collaborating with other organizations will show that we do not only care about ourselves but about others as well. Volunteering at shelters or places where people and animals are in need will show that us Muslims are kind hearted people. Not only will this show we help others but it will allow ourselves to earn more good deeds. Personally I have gone to feed the hungry with my dad and not only did it satisfy the children and families but it helped me notice that small actions like these that we take can make a big difference in someone's life.

In conclusion, the more we help out and work as an ummah the better people will see us. It is our job as Muslims to take care of ourselves and make sure we set the rules for what we are. We should not let anyone or anything determine what kind of people we are. I definitely know that I will not let anyone's comments affect me and that I will work hard and change how people see Muslims for the good of the ummah.

Faith in Action

**Consider how the early Muslims and today's faith-based communities overcame their contemporary social challenges; write an essay to identify the services/actions Musliums in America can undertake to address the social challenges of today. Use Surah Ihsan (verses 7-9) as your guide.
Please provide historical examples and practical strategies/actions to address the issues under current socio-political context.**

FIRST PLACE
Huma Chowdhury, College Park, Md.
Al Huda School

We live in a world of ignorance. Over 1400 years ago, people lived in a world of ignorance. Suspicion, bigotry, and fear filled the hearts of many, and it's almost as if nothing has changed today. Fortunately, it was the Prophet Muhammad and the message of Islam that lessened the uncertainty and fear that rested in people's hearts. Unfortunately, there were still many people who were relentless and determined to fight the Prophet and his followers.

From thorns being thrown in his pathway to severe torments and suffering in the scorching sun. The Prophet Muhammad and his followers endured endless amount of pain from those who had a lack of knowledge, hate, and prejudice against them. It was never easy for them to practice their deen openly because of the constant suspicion and discrimination they had to face.

Today, Muslims all over the world are facing issues that are almost identical to those faced by the Prophet Muhammad and his companions. In the contemporary world, dealing with media is almost the same conflict. A majority 55% (1) says that life has become more difficult after terrorist attacks. Muslims are left to face the fear, bigotry, and discrimination displayed by the public. Sadly, these problems we face today are not new and it is not just Islam that has had to go through this. In fact, other faith-based groups such as Judaism and Christianity went through rough social challenges as well. Intolerance was guaranteed for all these groups.

Islam, Judaism, and Christianity have all dealt with forms of inequity and discrimination as a result of ignorance. Although it happened many years ago, it continues to exist today. So, if these events continue to reoccur, what is it that we need to do in order to address these social challenges?

I can still remember my first encounter with intolerance when I was just 9 years old. My sister, father, and I went on our daily bike ride around the neighborhood. However, there was something different about this time. My older sister had just started wearing the hijab. I didn't think anything of it and especially didn't expect other people to have a problem with it either. But, as soon as we biked up to a stop sign, I remember hearing a stern, loud voice telling my sister, "Get off my property before I call the police". It wasn't like we were standing on his sidewalk. We were merely just passing by a neighborhood. My dad ignored it and told us to hurry along. At first, I didn't make the connection. Later on, I realized it was all because my sister was wearing the hijab. Something I thought was safe threatened another.

This is only one example of the many instances where hijabs are looked at for what they are not. In many cases, hijabs are actually pulled off, as it's been done to friends' of mine in school. Any instance where a person practices or shows their deen in public, risks being faced with this kind of bigotry and mistreatment.

As Muslims, the Prophet Muhammad portrays the best example to follow when dealing with these social challenges. We must follow through with what the Prophet characterized his Ummah with to shape his society in dealing with inequity. We must examine what the Prophet did in his time, reflect, and perform.

The first step in overcoming any challenge is having the belief and complete Tawakkul, or trust, in Allah. The Prophet Muhammad made it clear that the first thing all his followers did was put their complete reliance in Allah and leave it up to Him. For instance, when Abu Bakr was worried when the disbelievers were following them to the cave. The Prophet told him, "Don't be afraid, Allah is with us!" The first advice we need to learn to implement in our daily lives is to have this trust so that Allah can give us the patience when we need it the most.

After having full Tawakkul in Allah, it's important to understand that the Prophet (saw) didn't behave abruptly to overcome the injustice he was faced with. Rather, he worked on the Ummah and taught them the importance of unity, togetherness, and cooperation in times of need. Therefore, the second step is worship. The sole purpose Allah has created us is for His worship. The fact that we have the ability to worship in jama'a, together, teaches us something. It brings us closer to one another, and as it did in the past, increases the trust between individuals in the society. Having that strong bond between one another is what makes a difference. It is what the Prophet (saw) emphasized on, especially when they were faced with preconceived views from their enemies. (2)

The Prophet (saw) stressed the importance of knowledge and education. "Read." This was the first command given to the Prophet Muhammad. Allah tells us, "Say: 'Are those equal, those who know and those who do not know?' This ayah clearly tells us to take advantage of expanding our knowledge. The Prophet told us that those with knowledge are blessed, for it leads to the abandonment of ignorant traditions. Strengthening ourselves within the Ummah to free ourselves of any ties of being intolerant or prejudice is another important step we must take. Again, we must work on ourselves to persevere and make sure we aren't falling out of line. The Prophet (saw) put an end to the era of ignorance, replacing it with Islamic principles to follow. These rules and regulations forbade involvement in all injustices. The Prophet (saw) also taught the importance of cooperation in his principles. As we all know, "If one of you does not want for their brother in religion what they want for themselves, then they are not a true believer." Cooperation between one another and solidarity are some other characteristics that were taught to the companions, and should be practiced till this day.

First, we must begin with ourselves. This only works by worshipping Allah and having full trust in Him. Next, we must cooperate with our community members and the entire Ummah. We must work alongside others, and leave our differences, so that we can fight the injustices and ignorance together. Finally, we must educate ourselves. In order to perform the right services and actions, we must know what we stand for. When we know, Allah will help us better ourselves and better the community. Allah will allow us to become stronger so that we can successfully address the social challenges we face today. Yes, we live in a world of ignorance. And yes, it's as though we have been taken back to over 1400 years ago. But, we have the means to fix ourselves and follow the ways of the Prophet Muhammad. We have the means to overcome these challenges and make way for a better, educated future.

References:
1. Street, 1615 L., NW, Washington, S. 800, & Inquiries, D. 20036 202 419 4300 | M. 202 419 4349 | F. 202 419 4372 | M. (2011, August 30). Section 4: Challenges, Worries and Concerns. Retrieved from http://www.people-press.org/2011/08/30/section-4-challenges-worries-and-concerns/
2. What Changes did Prophet Muhammad make to the Society in which he Lived? - Ali Kapar, PhD. (n.d.). Retrieved January 16, 2017, from http://www.lastprophet.info/what-changes-did-prophet-muhammad-make-to-the-society-in-which-he-lived
3. Problems of the Second Generation: To be Young, Muslim, and American | Brookings Institution. (2001, November 30). Retrieved from https://www.brookings.edu/articles/problems-of-the-second-generation-to-be-young-muslim-and-american/
4. Part 3: Islam and Social Problems. (n.d.). Retrieved January 16, 2017, from https://www.al-islam.org/western-civilization-through-muslim-eyes-sayyid-mujtaba-musawi-lari/part-3-islam-and-social-problems
5. The Prophet and the people who opposed him | SoundVision. com. (n.d.). Retrieved January 16, 2017, from http://www.soundvision.com/article/the-prophet-and-the-people-who-opposed-him

SECOND PLACE
Afaaf Ahmad, Lanham, Md.
Home School

As we countdown the days to the inauguration of our 45th president, Muslims, and other minorities in the US and around the globe are all asking the same question, "What's going to happen now?" Now more than ever, Muslims in the US are facing challenges like Islamophobia, stereotyping, xenophobia, and hate. On a global scale, Muslims are facing what feels like some of the worst times in history, and the global community is dealing with morality at an all time low, and atheism on the rise. The entire Ummah is running into issues like disunity, Muslims losing their religion, and the so called radical Islam. We are facing an international epidemic that has plagued the Muslim community, serving as an obstacle and distraction hindering us from bringing about change. Though the whole world seems to be in shock of this newest challenge of our soon-to-be commander in chief, these challenges, and many others have already been encountered by the early Muslims and other faith based communities, and addressed in manners in which are lessons for us to follow. In order for us to overcome the social challenges presented to us as American Muslims, and as a society at large, we must reconnect ourselves to our religion by taking on certain mindsets, educate others, and engage in social and political activism.

The first and perhaps most important service we, as American Muslims can do for ourselves and our society is to reconnect ourselves to our all encompassing religion, and create the right mindset and outlook for ourselves, which starts off with our character. In numerous ahadith, the Prophet (saw) describes the best person as the one who "has the best manners and character", "is the best to his family", and "pays the rights of others generously". Another mindset a believer must embody, which is mentioned over thirty times in the Quran, is that of reliance on Allah (swt), or tawakkul. When we learn to rely on Allah (swt) alone, the fear that is associated with those other than him disappears, and we are able to take on any challenge that comes our way, due to our confidence in Allah (swt). When the Prophet (saw) and his companions were completely surrounded by the ahzab in the battle of the trench; a battle where their opponents outnumbered the Muslims 4:1, some of the hypocrites came to the Prophet (saw), and the Muslims and said: "The people have gathered against you; so, fear them", but as Allah (swt) says It increased them in Faith and they said, "Allah is fully sufficient for us, and the best One in whom to trust." (Al-Quran, 3:173). This mindset of tawakkul is what saved Ibrahim from the fire, and helped the early Muslims overcome the challenge of their time; the army of the disbelievers.

In Surah Insan, Allah (swt) says when defining the slaves of Allah (swt), "They (are the ones who) fulfill their vows, and fear a day whose evil (events) will spread far and wide." (Al-Quran, 76:7) This Ayah alludes to the final mindset that we must take on, which is constantly keeping the Day of Judgment at the front of our minds when making any decision, and especially while dealing with people and trying to bring about change. When Muslims in America internalize these qualities, and take on these mindsets, we can better equip ourselves to face the challenges that come our way in responsible and successful ways In shaa Allah.

Malala Yousafzai, a young girl who used the power of education to try to overcome the challenges facing her, said: "There are many problems, but I think there is a solution to all these problems; it's just one, and it's education." When speaking about facing challenges, education is one the most important services the Muslim community can partake in to overcome any and all challenges. In our communities and the global community at large, we feel the thirst for true, authentic education not only for our children, but for the elders as well. The amount of ignorance that has spread throughout our communities is sickening, and begs for solutions. This education not only includes giving Da'wah, which we cannot undermine, but also education about common social problems which are rising, and practical solutions for them. Muslims should be at the forefront in addressing social challenges by taking the lead in services such as family counseling, providing informative seminars on pertinent issues such as the dangers of social media, health seminars and other issues facing youth today. We need contemporary American Muslims in fiqh and shari'ah, in public relations, and in the film and social media industries, because these forms of education are what will truly change the hearts and minds of individuals around the planet.

As Muslims living America, we have a great responsibility to carry on our shoulders that we cannot let go of. We cannot afford to sit back with our heads in Canada watching what will unfold around the world! As long as we do our part, we belong here and we are here to stay. Muslims in America have to take part in the society to the fullest extent, not only locally, but globally. Every human being has his or her own capabilities, and can make a difference at all levels. Whether it be donating to charity organizations, or organizing a charity event ourselves, everything counts. When the African American community in the United States was faced with clear discrimination, the approach they used to overcome it was an action filled approach which challenged the social norms, yet proved effective and helped improve their status drastically. Though the Muslim community in the United States may not be facing that extent of challenges we can still be involved in social activities that not only address our problems, but the problems facing the society at large. Participating in rallies, petitions, and on the ground services to our fellow humans can all help solve the problems people are facing. Though we may undermine our likelihood of getting involved politically, that is a very effective way to help overcome the challenges faced by the local, as well as the global community. As Americans, we have the right to run for office, and should take advantage of this for the sake of the society, as our Muslim Senators, congressman, and other government officials have. When the Muslim community in the U.S. has our "act" together, we will, In shaa Allah, be able to overcome the challenges we face no matter large they may seem.

Allah (swt) says in the Quran: "Do you think that you will enter Paradise while you have not yet been visited by (difficult) circumstances like those that were faced by the people who passed away before you? They were afflicted by hardship and suffering, and were so shaken down that the prophet, and those who believed with him, started saying: "When (will come) the help of Allah?" (Then, they were comforted by the Prophet who said to them) 'Behold, the help of Allah is near.'" (Al-Quran, 2:214). Looking at the news, and swallowing global facts can get very depressing, but in the end we must understand that this world was never meant to be easy. We are simply travelers, walking along the well trodden path of life, brushing off the trials we face with forbearance and patience. Our mission here is not to overcome, but to try our best, for Allah (swt) is the only entity who will judge our effort, rather than the result. We must understand that with the right mindset, and through education and activism, Muslims in America have the power to rock the way we move forward as a human race, therefore we must seize this opportunity and never give up no matter how tough the going gets, for Allah (swt) reminds us in Surah Sharh: "So, undoubtedly, along with hardship there is ease. Undoubtedly, along with hardship there is ease. So, when you are free (from collective services), toil hard (in worship), and towards your Lord turn with eagerness." (Al-Quran, 94:5-8)

References:
1. "The Battle of the Trench." Last Prophet Muhammad (saw). N.p., 01 Jan. 1970.
2. "Hadith - Book of Virtues and Merits of the Prophet (pbuh) and His Companions - Sahih Al-Bukhari." Sunnah.com - Sayings and Teachings of Prophet Muhammad (saw). N.p., n.d.
3. "Malala Yousafzai Quotes." BrainyQuote. Xplore, n.d.
4. The Noble Quran: English Translation of the Meaning and Commentary.
5. Qadhi, Yasir. "Muslims in Trump's America: On the Eve After the Election ~ Shaykh Dr Yasir Qadhi." YouTube. YouTube, 10 Nov. 2016.

THIRD PLACE
Daiyan Musabbir, College Park, Md.
Al Huda School

Being a Muslim that is living and growing up in America comes with a variety of challenges and circumstances that we have to face on a daily basis. In this day and age, Muslims are often perceived as terrorists or as having a radical faith. The Prophet (saw) was sent down with the best religion and now our ummah is faced with a time of great challenges and hardships that we have to overcome.

Now, we cannot overcome any of these problems without understanding the reason for this critical view on our faith. What is the cause that has led them to see us in the negative light that they do? Such incidents are, for example, the 9/11 bombing, the Boston Marathon bombing, the shooting in Florida, etc; which are all tragic events done by people who claim Islam as their religion, and this skews the perspective of what Islam really is. We as a Muslim ummah in America face many difficult external and internal challenges such the Prophet (saw) did during his time, but in different circumstances and situations. Our goal should be to follow the example of the Prophet (saw) and the is the only way we will be able to handle our situation(s) the correct way.

Discrimination – the unjust or prejudicial treatment of different cate-gories of people or things, especially on the grounds of race, age, or sex. This may be one of the biggest challenge that we face; having an effect on us physically and psychologically. Our sisters shouldn't have a fear of their hijabs being snatched, as well as brothers shouldn't second guess their job options due to the fact that they want to follow the sunnah of Prophet, for example, keeping a beard or cuffing their pants. How do we deal with gruesome reality of the chances of being attack for your beliefs? Or we might be attacked verbally? The prophet (saw) was discriminated, mistreated, abused, and treated unjustly for 13 years in Makkah. He and the companions migrated to Madinah with nothing because of the cruelty of the makkans. Allah (Swt) told him in the Quran: "You will certainly hear much abuse from the followers of previous books and from the idol-worshipping people. And if you are patient and keep your duty -- this is surely a matter of great resolution." (Al-Quran, 3:185)

The problems Muslims face aren't only limited to this community, but many faith-based communities face the same issues that we do. They are affected with discrimination and prejudice resembling the issues we face, and in must be a collective effort from everyone to deal with these social challenges and obstacles so that we may overcome them.

Discrimination isn't just a problem that exists outside of Islam, it is also well indeed persistent in the folds of our own Muslim communities too. Due to the difference in skin tone, wealth, and social status people have a tendency to feel like as if they are superior than others. Allah does not judge according to our wealth or race but rather he judges according to the person's taqwa. This problem is adamant not only in our time. but was also adamant in the Prophet's (saw) time and it was solved by eradicating the ignorance in people's hearts and by increasing the amount of brotherhood between the muslims. In order to exterminate the issues that fester in the Muslim communities worldwide, we should fix these issues in our own community and thereafter we should expand this ideology of having everyone actually working together towards one goal rather than having the thought that "oh, the masjid administration will do it" . Although it might be hard to grasp, these problems can be solved on the dinner tables of Muslim families by having progressive conversations about these issues. Allah shows us in his book that we are all equal as he says: "O mankind! We created you from a single pair of a male and a female, and made you into nations and tribes that you might get to know one another. Surely the noblest of you in the sight of Allah is he who is the most righteous. Allah is All-Knowledgeable, All-Aware." (Al-Quran, 49:13)

The absence of a sense of brotherhood is a problem that branches from the discrimination in our communities. We do not have that sense of brotherhood that the companions had and this causes weak bonds in our community. When we see our brothers and sisters being killed, or being harmed overseas some of us don't even have sympathy for them at all. The Prophet (saw) said: "Love for your brother what you love for yourself." We should be willing and eager to help our brothers and sisters in any way they need, but we must remember why we are doing it. It is all for the sake of Allah (swt) and it is to please him, so that we may enter Jannah, as mentioned in surah Insan: "And they give food in spite of love for it to the needy, the orphan, and the captive, [Saying], "We feed you only for the countenance of Allah. We wish not from you reward or gratitude." (Al-Quran, 76:8-9)

These ayaat remind us that we must be sincere in all our actions regardless of how small the deed is. The only way we will overcome our trials and tribulations is by fearing and having trust in him, and making sure that our intentions are sincere.

Our internal problems that we deal with come from the pressures of the society we live in. Things which are not permissible in Islam have become a norm in society, and many of the youth have been exposed to it from a young age. Staying on the straight path may seem very difficult when you see guys your age are listening to music, hanging with the opposite gender, partying, etc. and then you have to hold your desire at that moment and remember why we are in this world. All of it is temporary. But being a Muslim was not meant to be easy. You will be tested to your limits; just remember, anything that comes your way is within your capacity to handle. "Do the people think that they will be left to say, "We believe" and they will not be tried?" (Al-Quran, 29:2)

In conclusion, Allah does not burden a soul more than it can handle. So all these issues and challenges are tests from Allah and if we stay steadfast on our deen and ask Him for help, these problems will become easy and we can overcome them like our predecessors have. "Verily, with every difficulty comes ease" (Al-Quran, 94:5)

References:
1. Abbas, Jamshed. Challenges facing Muslims in North America. (n.d.) Retrieved from https://crescent.icit-digital.org/articles/challenges-facing-muslims-in-north-america

2018

Alhamdulillah,
I Am a Muslim

Essay Panel Contest

2018

This poster was submitted by Sarah Imam in the Level 1 competition.

ELEMENTARY SCHOOL, LEVEL 1
Grades 1 & 2

Alhamdulillah, I am a Muslim

**Write a letter to your friend,
explaining what does it mean
to be a Muslim.
Tell him/her some of the things you do
at home and at school as a Muslim.
Don't forget to say also what makes
you proud to be a Muslim.**

FIRST PLACE
Saad Mahfuz, Greenbelt, Md.
Homeschool

Assalamu Alakium Ismaeel,

A few days ago, my teacher asked me about what it means to be a Muslim. So I thought it would be nice to share with you what I told her.

Being a Muslim means we have to obey Allah by praying. Since I was a little kid I saw my parents and brothers stand together for the five daily prayers. From what my brother tells me, I used to pray next to him and copy everything he did. I still pray now, and hope that you and I can pray together sometime. That way we can get good deeds from Allah together.

Next, it is important that Muslims respect prophet Muhammad (saw) by following what he used to do. The prophet Muhammad (saw) taught us a dua before sleeping, so every night before I close my eyes I say the dua. There are many more duas that the prophet taught us. So next time I see you we can learn some together.

The last thing I wanted to tell you about what it means to be a Muslim is listening to your parents and elders. To help my parents I sometimes do chores like doing laundry with them I also help my brothers by bringing them water bottle when they are busy with their own work. I love helping all of them!

Ismaeel, I am proud to be a Muslim because doing all these good deeds will make Allah happy. We should do more good together so we can make Allah (swt) happy and be in Jannah in shaa Allah.

SECOND PLACE
Zaheen A Pathan, Laurel, Md.
ICCL Academy

12340 Main Street
Someville MD 20777
January 10, 2018

Dear friend,

My religion is Islam, I worship one god and I believe Prophet Muhammad is his messenger. To be a Muslim means to be good, be happy, pray 5 times a day, and share with others.

As a Muslim I do many good things at school and at home. I make people laugh, I don't cheat, and I follow class rules. I read Quran which is our holy book, I say Salaam Alaikum which means peace, I respect my elders, and I help others.

I am proud to be a Muslim because many great inventions are made by Muslims. In my school I wrote about Al-Zahrawi and I did a project on him. He was a Muslim doctor. He invented many medical tools that save thousands of lives every day till today.

So, to be a Muslim means to be good and help others. I am proud to be a Muslim. Thank you for reading my letter.

Your friend

THIRD PLACE
Mustafaa Ahmed, College Park, Md.
M&M Learning Center

December 30, 2017

Dear Abubakar,

Assalamu Alakium. How are you? I have been thinking about why I am proud to be a Muslim. Do you even think about that?

You know, I am very happy that I believe in Islam. My parents are also Muslim, so they taught me to believe in Allah because he is the one that made everything.

Allah made the beautiful world, so we have to be thankful to him. My dad says that some people think that the world just came about by itself. To me, that's silly because something or someone had to create it. That had to be Allah.

There are many things I do in my daily life as a Muslim. At home, I listen to the Adhan and then I pray. I obey my parents and don't talk back to them. At school I always say Assalamu Alakium to everyone.

I respect my teachers too. I also always make wudu so I can pray anytime. In my community, especially during Ramadan, I help to make iftar bags. All of these things remind me that I am a Muslim and I am doing everything Allah wants me to.

Finally, I am proud to be a Muslim because Allah promises us Jannah if we follow his commands and be a good person. Allah says in surah Bakarah, ayah 82, "and those who believe and do righteous good deeds, they are dwellers of paradise and dwell there in forever." This is the goal for all Muslims.

Abubakar, can you tell me what makes you proud to be a Muslim? Write back soon.

Your friend

Essay Panel Contest

2018

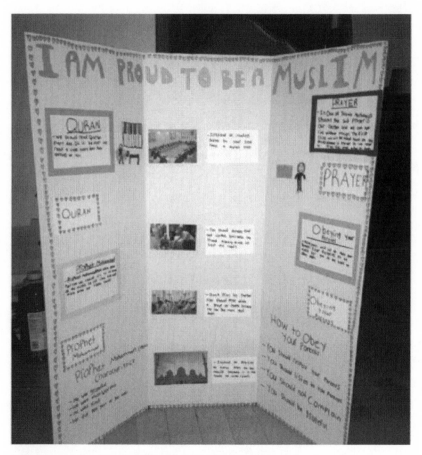

This poster was submitted by Huda Nassar in the Level 2 competition.

ELEMENTARY SCHOOL, LEVEL 2
Grades 3 & 4

Alhamdulillah, I am a Muslim

Identify something you say and do at your home and outside as a Muslim. How do you think these actions are benefiting you? Are you proud and thankful of your Muslim identify? Why?

FIRST PLACE
Zakariya Faisal, College Park, Md.
Al Huda School

There is a soft spot inside everyone. Omar's (ra) story is one example. One day, Omar woke up wanting to kill the Prophet (saw). He went out with his sword. On his way, he met a Muslim. The Muslim asked, "Where are you going"? He replied, "I am going to kill the Prophet." The Muslim said, "Why don't you deal with your family first?" Omar was mad. He went to his sister's home and heard them reciting Surah Taha (Al-Quran 20:1-7). He barged in. He hit his sister, but when he saw the blood he felt bad. He asked, "What were you reading?" After he made wudu and read the verses, he went to the Prophet. The Prophet said, "O Omar, isn't it time you become Muslim?" [1] Omar became Muslim. All the Muslims publicized that they were Muslims. Omar became Muslim from hearing 7 verses. Today, Allah has blessed us with 6236 verses. This Quran is the most valuable gift I have. And that's why I am proud to be a Muslim.

Alhamduillah, I am proud to have the words of Allah, the one who created this galaxy. The words of Allah tell me how to keep my body pure. Allah tells us not to eat pig. They roll in mud and can eat dung. Sharks are haram because they are carnivores. They might have eaten something haram. Allah tells us to keep our bodies clean by making wudu. We can't pray with something bad on us.

Alhamdulillah, I have a special day every week on Friday. Ibn Al-Qayyim said, 'It is a day of 'Eid that is repeated every week" (Zaad al-Ma'aad, 1/369). My favorite thing about Jumuah is the khutbah that tell about things we can implement in our lives. After Jumuah, people greet each other, we get to see our friends, and have delicious food. I am happy to see lots of people because when you pray you get good deeds multiplied by all those people.

Alhamdulillah, I am proud to be a Muslim because I have a unique time of the year, Ramadan. I love going to the masjid with my family at night, saying salaams to lots of people, praying Isha, going to childcare, and rolling up the mats. On 'Eid, I wake up early and prepare for the joyful day. On our way to the Salah, we loudly recite the takbiraat: Allahu akbar, Allahu akbar, Allahu akbar, laillaaha illa Allah. My heart feels very cheerful seeing loads of people following Allah's command. After I perform salah, I embrace my friends with three hugs. When we leave we take a different route, so that we can see more friends.

To me, brotherhood and the Quran are the most important things in my life as a Muslim. I have brothers in two ways - brothers in blood, and brothers in Islam. Alhamdulillah, I have a whole Muslim Ummah that I can rely on and can help me any time I am in need.

References:
1. Menk, Mufti Ismail. (2014, Ramadan). The Story Of Umar Ibn Khattab. Retrieved from https://www.youtube.com/watch?v=YHrJhnM35-w

SECOND PLACE
Hafsah Khan, Elkridge, Md.
Tarbiyah Academy

A few weeks ago, my mom and I were at the store and a lady in a wheelchair dropped her credit card on the ground. I bent down and gave it to her and she was thankful. Being helpful and caring is an example of what Muslims should do inside and outside of our homes. The Prophet (saw) said: "...Whoever solves someone else's problem, Allah will make things easy for him in this world and the Hereafter " (Muslim, 36) When my mom is in the kitchen, I try to ask her if she needs help. It makes me feel good when I help my mom because the Prophet (saw) has told us that jannah lies at the feet of your mother (Ahmad, 3104).

When I go to school everyday, I say "Assalam u alaikum" to my teacher and my friends. "Assalam u alaikum" means peace and blessings be upon you. Some Muslims say "hi" or "hello" which doesn't have a special meaning like "Assalam u alaikum" does. When someone says "Assalam ualaikum", it makes me feel closer to them. The Prophet (saw) said: "...Shall I not tell you about something which, if you do it, you will love one another? Spread salaam amongst yourselves." (Muslim, 54)

The most important thing that I do inside and outside of the house is worship Allah. We can do dhikr or make a simple du'a before we travel, eat, sleep and when we wake up. We can pray anywhere - it doesn't matter if we are inside or outdoors. This summer, we were driving to Texas and it was time to pray- we stopped at a rest area, made wudu, and prayed in the grass. Prayer benefits me because it helps me to remember Allah swt and thank Him swt for all of the blessings He has given me.

Why am I proud to be a Muslim? Because Allah swt has told us that He swt has perfected our religion of Islam (Al-Quran 5:3). Who wouldn't want to be a part of what is the best, or what is perfect? I love being a Muslim because I can talk to Allah swt whenever I want - I can even pray and make dua in my own bedroom. I can talk to Allah swt when I am happy or sad. I am happy to be a Muslim because I have the Quran which tells me everything I need to know, including how to behave, and all about the Prophets of Allah swt.

As a Muslim, there are many things that I do inside and outside of my home. I help others and I help my parents, I spread salams, and most importantly, I worship Allah swt. I am proud to be a Muslim because Islam is the most perfect and true religion. Also, Allah swt has given us the quran as a guidance in our lives, and He swt has given us so many other blessings. Alhamdulillah, I am proud to be a Muslim.

References
1. Hadith (Muslim, #36)
2. Hadith (Ahmad, #3104)
3. Hadith (Muslim, #54)

THIRD PLACE
Maheen Kamal, Baltimore, Md.
Al-Rahmah School

What makes me a Muslim? Why am I proud to be a Muslim?

Alhamdulillah, I am a Muslim and I am proud to be one. But what makes me a Muslim? Just because I am born to a Muslim family makes me a Muslim? Does my caramel colored skin make me a Muslim? Or the way I dress make me a Muslim? The simple answer to all these questions is that my belief and acts make me a true Muslim.

As a Muslim I must follow the five pillars of Islam. First, I need to say the Shahadah and not only say it but also believe in the concept of Tawheed, or the oneness of Allah and accept Muhammad (saw) as the last prophet. I should perform Salah five times a day. Fasting in the month of Ramadan makes the third pillar of Islam. My family also gives Zakat to the poor. And one day, In shaa Allah, I plan to travel to Makkah in the month of Dhul Hijjah to perform Hajj. I believe in Arkaan-ul-Iman, the belief in the prophets, angels, books of Allah, Day of Judgement, and fate determined by Allah.

Islam does not differentiate anyone based on their skin color, country of origin, or social class. The Prophet Muhammad (saw) made this clear in his last sermon at Mount Arafat on the day of Hajj by saying that an Arab has no superiority over a non-Arab, nor does a non-Arab have any superiority over an Arab; a white has no superiority over a black, nor does black have any superiority over a white; except by piety and good action. So, if I was white or black, I could still be a Muslim. Even if I was born in North Korea, Russia, or Djibouti, I could still be a Muslim. I could be born to the royal family of Brunei or the slums of Guatemala but still be a Muslim. I may be dressed in the finest silks and velvets, or the cheapest cotton, but I can still be a Muslim. The only obligation is modesty. In the eyes of Allah we are all equal except those with Iman. As the Holy Quran mentions: "We made you into nations and tribes, that you may know one another. Verily, the most honorable of you is the believer who has Taqwa." (Al-Quran 49:13)

I am proud to be a follower of such a beautiful religion which promotes diversity, dignity, and harmony in society. A belief that is based on truth and honesty which rewards good deeds here and hereafter. I am proud to be a Muslim because I follow Allah's deen which He Himself chose for us as He mentioned in the Quran, "On this day I have perfected your religion for you, completed My Grace upon you, and have chosen Islam for you as your religion." (5:3)

I believe that all Muslims should be proud of their Islamic faith despite the challenges that we as Muslims face daily.

References:
1. Soundvision.com
2. Authentictauheed.com

Essay Panel Contest

2018

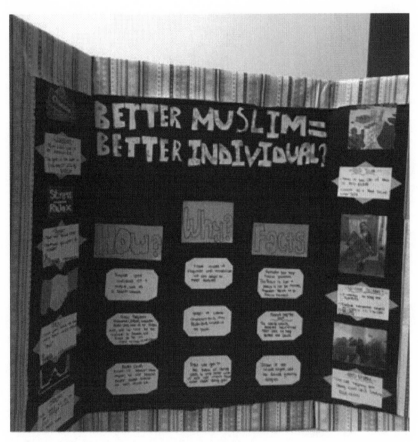

This poster was submitted by Jannah Nassar in the Level 4 competition.

Alhamdulillah, I am a Muslim

How do I demonstrate that being a Muslim, makes me a better individual in my school, family, and the community I live in? It's not always easy to maintain Muslim identity with all the negative incidents, news and attitude around us. Think about how you can encounter these negativities with your own words and actions as a Muslim. In particular, how do you think, by becoming a better Muslim you can be a better individual in your school, family, and the community you live in. How do you think it will boost up your morale and confidence as a Muslim?

FIRST PLACE
Khadijah Samiya, Greenbelt, Md.
Greenbelt Middle School

Rumi once said, "When someone beats a rug with a stick, he is not beating the rug – his aim is to get rid of the dust. Your inward is full of dust from the veil of 'I'-ness…With every cruelty and every blow, it departs little by little from the heart's face." Hardships are a means of cleansing ourselves. We constantly hear about negative incidents: acts of terrorisms in the false name of our peaceful religion, resulting in racial profiling, family homicides within our communities, bullying within our schools, and the list drags on. But we cannot let it drag on. Allah says, "Do the people think that they will be left to say, "We believe" and they will not be tried?" (Surah 29, Ayah 2). We as Muslims need to take action through these trials by having tawakkul, sabr, and ikhlaas.

I was bullied in school. An only hijabi in a sea of ponytails, braids, and afros, I was identifiably Muslim. I remember crying to my mom when I was mocked for my headscarf. "Are you gonna bomb the place?" "What are you hiding in there?" My mom consoled me, "Allah does not burden a soul beyond that it can bear" (Surah 2, Ayah 286). You control the power of the bullies." Who were these bullies? Not my friends or classmates; just people in the hallways with too much time in the 5 minutes between classes. The next day was a repeat of the previous day. Except I didn't cower back. Except I walked past with my head held high. I ran for Student Government and became the school's secretary. I used my power to start various initiatives. A designated safe space for Muslim students and staff to pray. A hall monitor program that ensured students were not engaging in wrongful behavior so that no one would relive what I had experience.

The number of students who told me that the program made them feel safe, was the reward I worked for. I effectively took power away from these bullies. My experience made me a better Muslim, strengthening my Eemaan and empowering me to take action when I see something wrong. Whenever you face a difficulty in school, remember to have tawakkul. He put you in this difficulty and He will pave the road out of it.

"Families are like fudge - mostly sweet, with a few nuts." We all struggle with our families but our Prophet struggled the most. His own uncle, Abu Lahab, didn't believe in the message he brought and worked to stop Islam from spreading. Abu Lahab ordered his two sons, the son-in-laws of the Prophet, to leave their wives. His wife placed thorns in the Prophet's path. Abu Lahab and his family did everything they could to destroy the Prophet. Yet, the Prophet persisted patiently and succeeded in carrying the torch of Islam. My struggles with my family are quite small compared to the Prophet's. My older sisters always pull the older sibling card. My parents have expectations higher than Mount Everest. It gets frustrating at times but it is because they know I can do better. My sisters may see something wrong that I can't understand and so I should trust their judgement when they tell me not to do something. Families require you to deal with patience, preferably in boatloads. Then again, the reward is equally immense as Prophet said, "Paradise lies at the feet of your mother."

Recently, we received pistachio macarons from our neighbor, in celebration of the holidays. Our neighbor is an old lady who had never before acknowledged our existence. We passed her house daily yet, it always felt like an empty house. This past Eid, we had shared our joy of the blessed day by sending her our special rice and meat, Biryani. Reflectively, I told my mom cheekily, "Fair trade: macrons for biryani." After chastising me, my mom reminded me of the true reason we shared -ikhlaas, desiring the sole pleasure of Allah. We shared because it is a form of da'wah. We shared because our neighbors have a right on us. We shared because on the Day of Judgement, we can say that we fulfilled their right on us. We shared to make Allah happy. Today, we interact with non-Muslims daily at our school, universities, and work. Due to the false accusations

Islam has acquired, people have an incorrect view and stereotype us in various forms. I cannot change people's opinions overnight. But my family's small acts of kindness can slowly but surely remove the mountain of ignorance the society has in regards to Islam. We need to take action with a sincere intention! Talk to your neighbors. Visit them when they are sick. Organize neighborhood cleanups, food drives, clothes drive, and anything that can help your community. You benefit as a Muslim because it is your sadaqah jariyah. Your community benefits with your acts of kindness. And just maybe, you change a few perspectives along the way.

I was bullied but I relied on Allah. I struggled with my family but I was patient. My community wasn't very welcoming, but I made sincere intentions. We all struggle with our school, family, and community, but the key solution lies in how we respond to them. As our individual rugs are beaten endlessly to rid our nafs of its dust, our hearts beat stronger with Rab - calling upon our Lord with every heartbeat for tawakkul, sabr, and ikhlaas.

References
1. "A Quote by Jalaluddin Mevlana Rumi." Quote by Rumi: "When Someone Beats a Rug with a Stick, He Is No..."
2. www.goodreads.com/quotes/1006668-when-someone-beats-a-rugh-with-a-stick-he-is.

SECOND PLACE
Nabeel Z. Chowdhury, College Park, Md.
Al-Huda School

What does it mean to be a true Muslim? According to the Webster's dictionary, a Muslim is a person whose religion is Islam. Islam is the religious faith of Muslims including belief in Allah as the sole deity and in Muhammad (saw) as His Prophet. As a young Muslim boy, I have been taught the five pillars of Islam and the six pillars of Imaan. Along with the words of the Quran, we are also taught to follow the ways of the Prophet Muhammad, such as being soft spoken, kind to others, and above all, forgiving and not being bitter towards people who throw negative comments towards us in today's society. The people who call themselves Muslim, but don't practice Islam are not really Muslim. True Muslims are those who portray righteousness throughout their school, family, and community.

As a Muslim, we can encounter the negativities being thrown at us from our society by demonstrating that true Muslims are better than what they are made out to be. The terrorists that are behind all the incidents such as killing, bombing, and shooting claim that they are Muslims, but they are not showing proof that they are true Muslims. If they don't practice true Islam, they cannot be true Muslims. Islam is a religion of peace. A true Muslim would never kill or even hurt anyone, as it says in Surah Ma'idah, Ayah 32, "…whoever kills a soul unless for a soul or for corruption [done] in the land - it is as if he had slain mankind entirely."

Let's say, a football player is saying that he is a good football player. Nobody would believe him unless he demonstrated that he is a good player. Similarly, if a person is a true Muslim, he must demonstrate it in his actions. A true Muslim prays salat 5 times a day, gives Zakat to the poor people, behaves well with others he knows, and so forth. A true Muslim refrains from speaking meaningless and immoral words, keeps himself away from pride, does not get involved in any bad activities, and so forth. The great Prophet (saw) has said, "Avoid which I forbid you to do and do that which I command you to do to the best of your capacity" (Bukhari and Muslim). These are a few ways a person could prove that he is a true Muslim.

As a better Muslim, we must learn to become a better individual in school, with our family, and within the community we live in. As a Muslim at school, we should pay attention to the teacher's notes while he or she is giving them, we should be disciplined while class is going on. We should encourage other classmates to pray salat at proper times, and make sure not to delay and procrastinate it. Finally, we shouldn't argue with our classmates or teachers when in school.

While we are with our family, we should stay calm and listen to anything that our relatives are saying. We should complete chores given to us by our parents and keep our relatives happy. We should encourage our relatives to practice Islam and we should show them how to by demonstrating. For example, we should be patient and grateful for whatever we have in our family. In Surah Anfal, Ayah 46, Allah says, "Indeed, Allah is with the patient."

Around our community, we could plant trees to keep our environment clean and green. We could set up trash cans, so people can stop throwing trash on the roads. We could visit houses and see if anyone is in need of service. As a true Muslim we must learn to be courteous towards others in the community and learn to respect others. We should also learn to get together as a community and hold fundraisers to raise money and awareness for those who are in need of money and other important causes.

Even though we live in a community full of negative attitudes towards Muslims, we should try to follow the path given to us by Allah and the Prophet Muhammad (saw). The world in which we live in is the ultimate test for the hereafter and Akhirah. The guidance that has been sent to us through the Quran and Sunnah is the best path for this test. Allah says, "Wealth and children are [but] adornment of the worldly life. But the enduring good deeds are better to your Lord for reward and better for [one's] hope." (Surah Kahf: Ayah 47). Following that path can make us a better Muslim, and thus, make us a better individual throughout our lives.

References:
1. Zainab, Abu. "20 Best Hadith to Make You a Better Muslim." Top Islamic Blog!, 12 Feb. 2013, http://topislamic.com/best-hadith/.

2. https://www.merriam-webster.com/dictionary Accessed 11 Jan. 2018.

3. "Knowing Sabr: 7 Quranic Verses About Patience." Quranic Quotes, https://quranicquotes.com/notes/quranic-verses-about-patience/. Accessed 11 Jan. 2018.

4. "Surah Al-Kahf [18:32-44]." Surah Al-Kahf [18:32-44], https://quran.com. Accessed 11 Jan. 2018.

5. "Surah Al-Ma'idah [5:32]." Surah Al-Ma'idah [5:32], https://quran.com. Accessed 11 Jan. 2018.

THIRD PLACE
Afrah Siddiqui, Greenbelt, Md.
Homeschool

It's after Isha prayer, the musllah is empty, and I'm playing hide and seek with my younger sister. There really isn't anyone there, just me and my family. All of a sudden, something stops me. Yesterday, I was working on my classwork in school and my friend asked me – "Are you a Muslim". I didn't really know exactly how to respond, so I did my best to change the subject. Being a Muslim is great, you get Eid presents, not once but twice every year, and you can always count on your Muslim friends; but being a Muslim isn't always so easy, and when you're asked if you are a Muslim, sometimes you can be hesitant. But while running around the musallah, I realized something. I am a Muslim, and I should be proud to be one. After all, it this faith that shapes me, makes me a better person. To me, a better person is someone who can make a positive impact in someone else's life. And that's exactly it, as a Muslim, I am taught to give charity, to be good to my parents; all these actions come from my religion, and make me a better person in my home and community.

First charity. Giving charity is an essential pillar of a Muslim's life. Charity, or to give, can come in many forms, not only money. Sharing what I know to my younger sister, for example, is charity; even smiling is charity, according to the Prophet (saw). In the Quran, Allah (swt) stresses the giving of charity many times "Those who in charity spend of their goods by night and by day, in secret and in public, have their reward with their Lord: on them shall be no fear, nor shall they grieve" (2:274).The Prophet (saw) said "Save yourself from Hell-fire even by giving half a date-fruit in charity." (Sahih al-Bukhari, Hadith 1417)   These just show that charity is a big part of Islam. By giving money to those in need in my community, those living without a roof on their head or food in their stomachs, I can be a better Muslim by saving myself from the punishment of the hell-fire, and can have a positive impact on someone else's life. Also, sharing my knowledge and experience, whether that be to my little sister, my friends in public school or Sunday school, I can make sure that I can have a positive impact. Likewise, even just smiling to those around me, saying "Hi" or "Salam Alaikum" with an exclamation point, I can possibly make their day. Alleviating problems of those in my community, school, and home make me a better Muslim and a better individual as I am able to gain the reward from Allah (swt), and be able to make a positive impact to those around me.

Second, being respectful to my parents can make me a better person. Being good to parents includes helping out in the kitchen, taking care of younger siblings, setting the table for meals, getting the mail and newspaper, taking out the trash etc. Allah (swt) and the Prophet (saw) emphasized the need of being good to your parents. For example in the Quran is "Worship Allah and associate nothing with Him and be good to parents." (Al-Quran 4:36) Narrated Abdullah ibn Amr Ibn al-'Aas " A man came to the Apostle of Allah (peace be upon him) and said: I came to you to take the oath of allegiance to you on emigration, and I left my parents weeping. He (the Prophet) said: Return to them and make them laugh as you made them weep. (Sunan of Abu-Dawud , Hadith #2522). The evidence mentioned above demonstrates the importance of respecting your parents. Being respectful to my parents gains me rewards from Allah (swt) and also make me a better individual. This is because when I show them respect, it it I care about them and they are important to me, and also more importantly, I can make them pleased with me, thus making me a better person in my home.

All in all, charity, which including the sharing of money, knowledge, and even a smile, along with being good to parents are just a few of many examples of how I can become a better person in my school, community, and home. I continued to chase my sister in the musallah, but I learnt something; I am a Muslim and because of my faith, I am a better individual to people in my community, home, and school.

References:
1. (n.d.). Retrieved January 1, 2018, from https://sunnah.com/bukhari/24/21
2. Al-Qur'an al-Kareem (n.d.). Retrieved January 1, 2018, from https://quran.com/
3. Honor your father and mother in Islam. (2015, September 17). Retrieved January 1, 2018, from https://abuaminaelias.com/honor-your-father-and-mother-in-islam/
4. Parents. (2012, August 01). Retrieved January 1, 2018, from http://hadithoftheday.com/parents/

Essay Panel Contest

2018

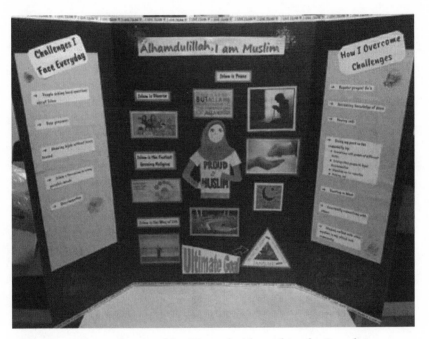

This poster was submitted by Noorah Ahmed in the Level 4 competition.

Alhamdulillah, I am a Muslim

How do I demonstrate that being a Muslim, makes me a better individual in my school, family, and the community I live in? It's not always easy to maintain Muslim identity with all the negative incidents, news and attitude around us. Think about how you can encounter these negativities with your own words and actions as a Muslim. In particular, how do you think, by becoming a better Muslim you can be a better individual in your school, family, and the community you live in. How do you think it will boost up your morale and confidence as a Muslim?

FIRST PLACE
Noorah Ahmed, College Park, Md.
Beltsville Academy

ALHAMDULILLAH, I AM A MUSLIM

How do I demonstrate that being a Muslim makes me a better individual in my school, family and the community I live in?

Finding the right path in life can seem easy when you are already born into a religion. For me, my entire family is Muslim, alhamdulillah, but it is better to figure out on your own whether what everyone believes is the right thing, especially when it comes to religion. I have contemplated how the world and I came to be and learning about Islam from my parents and my Muslim community have convinced me that Islam is not just the best religion, but it is the right religion. Islam is diverse, the most diverse religion in the world, which makes sense because a religion that is true would make sense to people of all backgrounds. Islam is the fastest growing religion, which demonstrates that there is something true about Islam that others are embracing. Islam is also the only religion that addresses what happens to all of creation once it ceases to exist, because neither we nor the world will be around forever. As a Muslim, with so many negative things happening all around me, Islam is the only thing that brings me peace. I feel at peace when I pray 5 times a day and when I make du'a. Alhamdulillah, I am proud to be Muslim, because it is a way of life for me, and my pride has shaped me as an individual and how I live my life.

The world is full of all kinds of challenges these days. For me, it is sometimes difficult to keep a good character when others are not being very friendly towards me. This is especially true since I go to a public school, where there is a completely different environment from my home and the Muslim community I am in. In the face of all the negativities, I try to keep my Muslim identity no matter what by practicing hijab, watching how I interact with different people, and who I surround myself with. I remain calm and try to see things from the other person's perspective. I try not to judge anyone. However, peer-pressure is always there, and like any other teenager, I don't want to be that much different from others. It is easy to consider removing my hijab when there is so much talk of terrorism and when the news puts Muslims in a bad light. Whenever this is a shooting or some kind of bomb attack, I worry that my friends will ask me why Muslims are doing these things. Some people stay away from me thinking that I believe in killing innocent people. These daily experiences can take a toll on me and make me wonder why Islam tells us to live a certain way that doesn't seem like much fun. However, because I was exposed to the Quran since I was very young, I know that Allah (swt) answers this question by saying in Surah Al-Ma'idah, ayah 3, " This day I have perfected for you your religion and completed My favor upon you and have approved for you Islam as your religion." This is Allah (swt) telling us He has perfected this way of life for us. No other religious text says this. The challenge for Muslims is to accept this and move forward by following all of the guidelines set forth by Allah (swt).

There are quite a few strategies we can use to overcome the negatives we face daily. I have constantly been told by my parents, Qur'an teacher, and from lectures, that our Salah and du'a are the most powerful weapons we have. While we are always trying to do our best in any situation, the only one who can turn things around is Allah (swt). When people are mean to me, and I am trying to be as nice as possible, I don't really see positive results in every situation. When I do call out to Allah and ask for His help, I do find that I feel less stressed and eventually it seems like the people being mean are out of my life or surprise me by being nicer. Another way to counter the negativities is to join a cause that is worthy of bringing to light injustices happening in our own communities or even around the world. I did not attend the Women's March that happened last year, but I saw it as a powerful way to get across a message. I felt empowered just knowing that so many people believed that there are many things that needed to be changed for the better, especially given the new President and his goals for America. Uniting with anyone who has a common goal towards positive outcomes is a good way to give dawah and show that Muslims are about humanity and compassion. This is also a great way to serve our communities.

At the end, Islam has a purpose. This world is not going to last forever. I believe my actions will benefit me by getting me closer to a place of eternal bliss--Jannah. We have been given the roadmap to achieve this. To me, by becoming a better muslim, I am not judging other people, trying to practice patience, being forgiving, being optimistic and compassionate towards others, taking care of the environment, and keeping my intentions for everything for Allah's sake. Allah (swt) says in Surah Ali Imran, Ayah 134, "Those who spend in the way of Allah both in plenty and hardship, who restrain their anger, and forgive others, Allah loves such good-doers." Finally, even though I was born into a muslim family, I still face challenges and hardships everyday. Life is tough, but I tell people that it is OK. Allah (swt) says in Surah Ali Imran, Ayah 142, "Did you think that you would enter paradise even though Allah has not yet seen who among you strove hard in His way and remained steadfast?" For me, this is worth going through all the hardships, Alhamdulillah.

SECOND PLACE
Mohammed Abdul Mujeeb, Laurel, Md.
Homeschool

Assalamualaikum,

Allah said in (Surah 4, Ayah 36) "Worship Allâh and join none with Him (in worship), and do good to parents, kinsfolk, orphans, Al-Masâkin (the poor), the neighbor who is near of kin, the neighbor who is a stranger, the companion by your side, the wayfarer (you meet), and those (slaves) whom your right hands possess. Verily, Allâh does not like such as are proud and boastful".

Islamic teachings have made me the person I am today. They have crafted my character and sculpted my manners. They have also taught me how to deal and behave around other people. I have been in situations in my school, family, and community where the way me being a Muslim affected my decision. Let me tell you about how I dealt with these situations in different scenarios.

Before we begin, I would like to clarify something. The topic asks us how we can be better individuals in our community, school, and family. Being a good human means being generous, kind, humble, peaceful, and other traits. A good Muslim also has these characteristics, but he/she has the intention to please Allah (swt). We are being asked how we can be better humans and better Muslims at the same time.

Let me start off with the community. I live in a community where the population is mostly non-Muslims. I have had many opportunities to help my neighbors. One instance is that whenever we make a special dinner, my mother saves some of the food and tells me to distribute it to the neighbors. Another situation is when my neighbor was moving, and the father moved early because of his job, and his wife was left alone to pack up everything. My father and I took this opportunity to help the family move furniture and disassemble heavy items. When the family started thanking us for helping them, we stopped them saying that it was our duty because as I mentioned in the ayah before, Allah says that we have to do good to your neighbor who is a stranger and also who is near of kin. Acts like these strengthen the bond between neighbors, and makes them respect us for who we are.

Another way to be a better individual in your community is by being active in the society. There are many ways we can do that. For example, my community held an event last year during the date of 9/11 and called the leaders of every religion to come say inspirational speeches. All of us remembered who was killed and we grieved for them as a community. I attended this event along with some other Muslims representing the Masjid. Doing this made the other religious members also attending the session know that Muslims were also socially active in our community.

In the ayah that I mentioned before, Allah tells us to do good to our parents and kinsfolk which means our family. How can I attend to my parents needs and wants on a daily basis? I do things that any kid would do to serve their parents. I make breakfast, take out the trash, mow the lawn all to serve my parents. What differentiates me from any other kid is my intention to please Allah. Parents have a high status in Islam and serving them is our duty.

Another thing that I noticed which could be applied to every aspect of this topic is that under the western influence, people have become so busy that don't even pray or they think that praying is not for people of their caliber. Instead telling them directly, praying in public places and calling when it is time for salah will influence them to start praying too.

In the Islamic school I went to, we were supposed to follow our Islamic lifestyle and beliefs. To encourage us, our school chose a characteristic like honesty or patience every month and gave us a certificate if we followed the characteristic for a whole month. My classmates and I competed with each other to see who would get the prize. These Islamic traits were engraved in us so we would be good Muslims throughout our life and we would also be good people to each other in school.

The reputation that we build is crucial to being better individuals. A reputation will leave an impression on the person such as "When I was in need, that Muslim kid came and helped me." A reputation will also become motivation for you and me to live up to it and even strive to do more.

Through this essay I hoped you learned something you could do to help your family, school or community. Thank you for your time.

THIRD PLACE
Safiyyah Baqqi-Barrett, Laurel, Md.
Baqqi Academy

Muslims today are not always viewed by others in a positive light, and there are many misconceptions about what it means to be a Muslim. Because of this, it can sometimes be hard for some Muslims to maintain a positive identity. It is important for Muslims to do things that build confidence and that show Muslims in a positive light to the rest of the world. I want people to know that being a Muslim makes me a better individual in my family and community because Islam encourages us to be merciful, just, and kind to our families, neighbors, friends, and others.

I have tried to show what it means to be a good Muslim in many ways. I often help my parents in taking care of the house by helping with chores and keeping it clean. I help with caring for my baby brother by watching out for him and helping to feed him. I also spend lots of time playing with him and my sister. This is how I show mercy and compassion to my family.

When I am with my Girl Scout troop, we try our best to give good dawah and follow The Sunnah by volunteering and putting forth the best image of what it means to be a good Muslim. We make sure to and really enjoy doing lots of community service during the year. I show that I am a Muslim by wearing my hijab, and when people see that I am a Muslim and a Girl Scout, this helps them to form a connection with me and the other girls in our troop.

I have many non-Muslim relatives and it is important for me to help them understand what being a good Muslim looks like. When my grandma visits, I make sure to help her with her bags and anything else she might need. I thank her sincerely for the gifts she brings us, and I am kind to her. When she is in our home, she only hears me speak kindly to my family and she sees how much I enjoy spending time with her and them. My grandma shared with my mom that she has told her fellow church members good things about our family, especially when one of them spoke negatively about Muslims. The nice things she said about us worked to change their minds and teach them something new about Islam.

Islam calls us to be better people by encouraging us to take care of our families, neighbors, and even those we don't know. By following the example of the Prophet Muhammad (saw), we only become stronger in our religion and we are able to be better Muslims, even when being a Muslim seems difficult. Our actions as Muslims have the power to both change how others see us and how we see ourselves.

Essay Panel Contest

2018

This poster was submitted by Shaheer Imam in the Level 5 competition.

Alhamdulillah, I am a Muslim

How do we keep the flame of faith alive? We're taught in the Qur'an and Sunnah that holding on to faith is a difficult task indeed. Allah tells the believers in the Qur'an: "Do not die, except that you are in a state of Islam." The Prophet told us further that there will come a time that "an individual wakes up as a believer, but begins the night as a disbeliever…" Our identity, pride, and confidence are being constantly hammered and attacked by negative campaign tactics with a clear target on our morale, spirit, and belief. Today, we are defined by others – we are stereotyped, our belief is portrayed as being obsolete and/ or extreme – the goal is simple: to shake our belief and confidence, question our identity, and to tear our unity apart.

FIRST PLACE
Sawdah Munir, Ellicott City, Md.
Mount Hebron High School

A Call for Unanimity

Often the revival and resurgence of a movement is attributed to the vigor with which the end goal is sought. However, change is not effective without harmony in action and thought. In order to keep the flames of faith alive and end stereotypes in the general public, our community at its heart must first be reevaluated. By retaining unity under a Muslim identity through elimination of prejudice and visitation of core values, we will strengthen a bond amongst ourselves that will allow us to overcome any obstacle or challenge we may face.

The idea of a Muslim identity is the realization that faith unites us at our core, no matter our heritage or ethnicity. We cannot dispel prejudice against ourselves if we hold it amongst one another. The Muslim community is a diverse entity spanning worldwide, a melting pot of different races and cultures. The United States of America is a prime example of how such a distinct society is able to coexist. Based on U.S. Census Bureau data, the Pew Research Center concluded that 41% of US Muslims are white, 28% are Asian, 20% are black, 8% are Hispanic, and 3% are other or mixed. Islam in America cannot be attributed to one single race or ethnicity. As noted by Andrea Elliot (2007), with the wave of immigrants hailing from South Asia and the Middle East in recent decades, the emergence of a cultural and racial divide was found between them and the indigenous African-American Muslims. From her interviews, Elliot (2007) gleaned that the tragedy of September 11, 2001 had united the Muslim community against prejudice, overriding racial boundaries for faith. Especially in recent years, the masjid communities have diversified, illustrating a rainbow of Muslims from all different origins (Eck, 2018). Even with this improvement, the struggle is not yet over; such a community must be maintained and fortified. Elliot (2007) eloquently notes that "the divide between black and immigrant Muslims reflects a unique struggle facing Islam in America. Perhaps nowhere else in the world are Muslims from so many racial, cultural and theological backgrounds trying their hands at coexistence. Only in Mecca, during the obligatory hajj, or pilgrimage, does such diversity in the faith come to life, between black and white, rich and poor, and Sunni and Shiite." By reaching this level of unity and love for one another, our iman as a brotherhood is invigorated. Dispelling racist sentiment also allows us to set an example to the world, a form of Da'wah, reinforcing our religion as that of peace not only by sentiment but also by actions. From Sahih Al-Bukhari, Abu Musa (ra) narrates that the Prophet (saw) said, "A believer to another believer is like a building whose different parts enforce each other." The Prophet (saw) then clasped his hands with the fingers interlaced (while saying that) (Bukhari, Vol. 3: Book # 46, Hadith #7). The Muslim identity is the building that Rasulullah (saw) describes. Each member must play their role to stabilize it and keep it standing. The endurance of our community lies in our ability to support one another, giving us the strength to define ourselves by our faith and not by the words of others.

Another vital aspect of our integrity as Muslims is re-establishing our faith as a lifestyle ingrained within us, rather than simply regarding it as the tradition of our parents and older generations. With the rise of hate groups intending to dismantle the tenacity of our faith, a Muslim's "life should ideally be a complete manifestation of his belief. Thus, whatever the environment, this testimony and life of the heart must be protected and respected" (Ramadan, 1999). When being a Muslim becomes a way of life, our confidence in our piety gives us the capacity to strengthen the morale of our peers, exemplifying what it means to be a believer, a follower of Islam. Our faith is what distinguishes us; a community, where each individual is steadfast in their relationship between themselves and Allah (swt), will prevail and overcome the challenges the dunya presents. The Qur'an reminds us that we are not alone in this endeavor, "God has inscribed faith upon their hearts and strengthened them with a Spirit from Him. He causes them to enter Gardens with rivers running below... They are the party of God. Truly the party of God - it is they who shall prosper" (Quran 58:22, The Study Quran). By following the Qur'an closely, we utilize a guide that can reinvigorate our lifestyles with faith, making our Akhlaq a shining example for not only teaching the ignorant but also cultivating other Muslims. This refocus into the core of our values allows for a unity in existence, a group of people with a common purpose. Being at peace with ourselves and with Allah (swt) means we can better convey these morals to those who may condemn or doubt us. We must first understand ourselves, and our identity as Muslims before we can hope that of anyone else.

Change is not a destination easily reached. Readjusting our mindset is only the first step to creating a meaningful difference, one that will encourage coexistence and acceptance between religions. Maintaining firm bonds and beliefs constructs a community prepared for revision, one that will not be swayed by the bitterness of hostile forces. There can be no resistance from a divided people.

References:
1. Eck, D., & Presidents and Fellows of Harvard College. (n.d.). Unity and diversity. Retrieved January 9, 2018, from The Pluralism Project website: http://pluralism.org/religions/islam/issues-for-muslims-in-america/unity-and-diversity/
2. Elliott, A. (2007, 11 Mar). Between black and immigrant muslims, an uneasy alliance. New York
3. Times (New York, NY) Retrieved from https://sks.sirs.com
4. Ramadan, T. (1999). To Be a European Muslim. Markfield, UK: The Islamic Foundation.
5. The Hadith, (pp. Sahih Bukhari, Book 46, Hadith 7).
6. U.S. muslims concerned about their place in society, but continue to believe in the american dream. (2017, July). Pew Research Center.

SECOND PLACE
Ayman Fatima, Laurel, Md.
Al-Huda School

Assalamualaikum,

"Difficult times are meant to bring you closer to the All-Mighty. So if you are having a rough day, be calm. Let His plan unfold." (Mufti Menk) The Muslim Ummah today is surrounded by a "fire" which is fueled by hatred and misconceptions of us Muslims and Islam. We have to fight back the negativity. But how? Becoming hotheaded and forming a group of Muslims to start a revolution without a game plan, is not the way. History proves that successful revolutions and lasting changes have been made when strong and determined individuals with a clear goal, congregated to make an invincible "army". Our Ummah has to learn from this. Once we cultivate ourselves to become sound individual Muslims, we can then join forces and fight back the detestation from the people around us.

Now, the next question arises. How do we refine ourselves to become strong? How do I reawaken the flames of faith within me? As we all know, physical fire needs three elements to ignite and remain: heat, oxygen and fuel. We can replace these elements with three vital steps for us to start and maintain a spiritual "flame". For our heat aspect, our first step would be to spend a few minutes daily to read a hadith or an ayah. For our oxygen element, our next step would be to constantly remind ourselves about Allah and the Aakirah, particularly about Jannah and Jahannam. For the fuel aspect, our last step would be to surround ourselves with pious Muslims to continuously get inspired from their positive influence and be motivated.

There is a famous saying, "A little goes a long way." That is especially true regarding our deeds. Allah mentions that He appreciates the deed that is small but is done consistently rather than a heavy deed done once, then forgotten. This means that the person who reads one page of Quran on a regular basis has more value in the eyes of Allah than the person who reads three juz one day and doesn't get back to the Quran until the next Ramadan. Relating back to our internal fire, we need the heat. Taking out less than 10 minutes from our hectic days to read a hadith or an ayah can give us an eeman refresher and get ourselves back in the zone. Scholars say that whoever does this act with a good intention, his day will be productive and Allah will protect him from all harms. We as Muslims definitely need the indemnity of Allah from the Satan that is behind all the stereotypes against us.

Some people excel when there is a reward at the end of their effort. Others do not. They need constant reminders of the consequences to keep them focused on their task. Allah presented to us both the reward (eternal life in Jannah) and the punishment (eternal life in Hellfire – 'auzubillah). This way anyone can look at themselves and see what pushes them to excel and be productive. Allah intricately describes the beautiful haven for the believers in the Quran (Al-Quran 47:15) "This is the description of Paradise, which the righteous are promised, wherein there are rivers of water unaltered, rivers of milk the taste of which never changes, rivers of wine delicious to those who drink, and rivers of purified honey, in which they will have from all [kinds of] fruits and forgiveness from their Lord." On the other hand, the terrors of the Hellfire are also prevalent. (Al-Quran 18:29) "...Indeed, we have prepared for the wrongdoers a fire whose walls will surround them. And if they call for relief, they will be relieved with water like murky oil, which scalds [their] faces. Wretched is the drink, and evil is the resting place." With the pleasures of Paradise and the horrors of Hellfire both presented to us, we can motivate ourselves to become more Allah-conscious, and eventually become able fight against society that portrays us as terrorists.

Mankind has been vulnerable to other people's influence, whether good or bad. A person's surroundings reflect their character and personality in all matters. We are known by the company we keep.

With this in mind, we should realize the significance of having pious Muslims and strong individuals within our proximity. We can accomplish this goal by being in the presence of scholars and imams while imitating the Sunnah of the Prophet, one step at a time. This ensures that we have no excuse to rely on when we didn't wake up for Fajr or when we forgot to say "Bismillah" before we ate.

With all this in mind, we cannot forget the fact that we all are human beings – the favorite creation of Allah. It is vital that whatever effort we are putting, that we are merciful and courteous whilst doing it. If we display rude behavior back to those who are rude to us, we are nothing but mirrors and there is no difference between them and us. Islam is the best of all religions. We were chosen to be Muslims. For us to make a make a crack in the shell of misconceptions, we need to have "fire" and determination. This inspiration to be the very best Muslim we can be, cannot be toppled by the bigotry and erroneous theories about Islam. When we have the firm belief that we will be the successful ones with Allah's help, there is no one that can hinder us from accomplishing our goals and pleasing Allah. So, let us all understand our responsibility as ambassadors of Islam and make sure that it is no longer portrayed as a religion of war, but a religion of peace.

References:
1. Lapowsky, I. (2013, April 2), "Reward vs. Punishment: What Motivates People More?" Retrieved from:
2. https://www.inc.com/magazine/201304/issie-lapowsky/get-more-done-dont-reward-failure.html
3. Kamil M. (2017, February 26) "A DESCRIPTION OF HELLFIRE" Retrieved from: https://www.islamreligion.com/articles/344/description-of-hellfire-part-1/
4. Scott, (2011, September 7) "How to Lead a Revolution: 8 Underused Tactics to Build a Massively Loyal Following" Retrieved from: https://liveyourlegend.net/how-to-lead-a-revolution-8-underused-tactics-to-build-a-massively-loyal-following/

5. Green, E. (2017, July 26) "How Much Discrimination Do
Muslims Face in America?" Retrieved from: https://www.
theatlantic.com/politics/archive/2017/07/american-muslims-
trump/534879/
6. Pirani, F. (2017, May 5) "Muslims in America, by the numbers"
Retrieved from: http://www.ajc.com/news/national/muslims-
america-the numbers/tJI0VhrVWDYQ1wCplHjozK/

THIRD PLACE
Mustafa Khalid, Greenbelt, Md.
Eleanor Roosevelt High School

Keeping the Flame of Faith Alive

"But whoever changes from good faith to disbelief has definitely
stayed away from the correct path" (Al-Quran 2:108). From this
ayah, it is clear that Iman or faith is necessary to stay on the path
of Islam. Today, in an Islamophobic world, the love of our faith has
been hammered down by schemes built to demoralize our identities
and ideals. These tactics have been a bulldozer to the faith of many
Muslims around the world. In order to keep the flame of faith alive,
we Muslims must adhere to the Quran and Sunnah, differentiate
ourselves from our peers and surroundings through our manners
and actions, and keep Taqwa in all our situations. By sticking to these
principles, Muslims can create a situation in which they not only
muster strong faith but also proudly display it and make themselves
the example to others.

As Muslims, our lives and ethics should wholly be based of the Quran
and Sunnah. The stress of these two important aspects are stated in
Surah Al Nisaa "... obey Allah and obey the Messenger...That is the
best way and the best in result" (Al-Quran 4:59). From this ayah
we see that the best path to take is the one set by the standards of
our Lord and the Prophet. Approaching this lifestyle, we see that
remembering Allah is the foremost way of approaching life as He

says in Surah Al-Baqarah "So remember Me and I will remember you"(Al-Quran 2:152). From this Ayah, we learn that keeping Allah in mind subsequently results in remembrance of Allah, the only true way and the most important aspect to succeed in faith. Following the Prophet is also stressed in the Quran as Allah says in Surah Al Nisaa "He who obeys the Messenger has obeyed Allah"(Al-Quran 4:80). These words clearly state that following Allah comes with following the Messenger. From these few among many Ayat that speak about following Allah and the Messenger, we can formulate the only way to form a foundation for a burning faith is to keep Allah and the Prophet's commands in hand. The flame of faith can only be ignited and kept torrid with this concept in mind.

One of the main problems of being a Muslim in this era and land is finding or creating a surrounding of good people of good attitude. The general ethics in this world clash with those we should follow in Islam. If we want to keep our faith intact, it is crucial we Muslims differentiate ourselves from those who surround us. The simplest way to do this is learn the deep mannerism we Muslims are commanded to follow. The stress of these manners are exemplified by great scholars of Islam such as Abdullah bin al Mubarak who said "I spent thirty years learning manners, and twenty years learning knowledge"(Mubarak). This quote clearly exemplifies the importance of mannerism in Islam. If we Muslims cannot follow a certain creed of conduct, we will not be different from those who surround us even if we have all the knowledge of the world. Our faith is not controlled by our words, but rather by our actions making it necessary to be mannerful. In order to attempt a mimic of what previously was in the Islamic world, we must keep our mannerism intact like the example of the Prophet who was called "The Truthful," "The Trustworthy," and described as the "Quran walking". From what we see in the greatest man to step onto the Earth, mannerism is a key component of the flame of faith.

Taqwa, or the fear of Allah is a key to keep the flame of faith burning. The implications of not having Taqwa in our lives are drastic as it is the shame that keeps us from staying away from the evils of this world. Taqwa compliments faith as it ties with belief in Allah as said in Surah Al-Hashr "Oh you who have believed, fear Allah" (Al-Quran 59:18). This ayah clearly indicates the connection between Taqwa and faith. Taqwa is clearly unachievable without faith as stated in the ayah. Strong Taqwa not only exemplifies good faith but it represents one's character in the toughest of situations. This love and fear for Allah counts toward a strong faith.

While the faith of many Muslims are being hammered constantly, our belief in Allah and His Messenger can help us if we confidently believe in it by establishing Taqwa and by molding our character into that follows the example of the Prophet. By following these points and through the will of Allah, we Muslims will one day succeed again.

Essay Panel Contest

2018

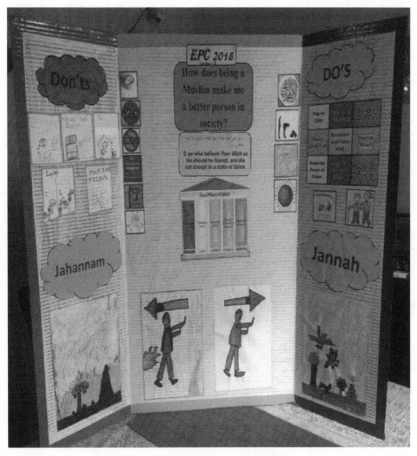

This poster was submitted by Ahmad Imam in the Level 3 competition.

Alhamdulillah, I am a Muslim

How do we keep the flame of faith alive? We're taught in the Qur'an and Sunnah that holding on to faith is a difficult task indeed. Allah tells the believers in the Qur'an: "Do not die, except that you are in a state of Islam." The Prophet told us further that there will come a time that "an individual wakes up as a believer, but begins the night as a disbeliever..." Our identity, pride, and confidence are being constantly hammered and attacked by negative campaign tactics with a clear target on our morale, spirit, and belief. Today, we are defined by others – we are stereotyped, our belief is portrayed as being obsolete and/ or extreme – the goal is simple: to shake our belief and confidence, question our identity, and to tear our unity apart.

FIRST PLACE
Adam Ahmad, Lanham, Md.
Homeschool

As a minority group living in a society where we are targeted, stereotyped, and looked down upon, where immorality and discrimination are on the rise, many Muslims are questioning their faith, and even leaving it behind out of lack of social integration. Allah tells us the benefits of faith in Surah Hadeed, where He says, "O you who have believed, fear Allah and believe in His Messenger; He will [then] give you a double portion of His mercy and make for you a light by which you will walk and forgive you; and Allah is Forgiving and Merciful." (Al-Quran 57:28) Allah has also told us repeatedly in the Quran that he is the protector and close ally of those who have faith. Keeping the flame of faith alive and strong is a lifelong process that we must undertake with patience and perseverance, and the most significant steps we can take towards this journey are changing our way of thinking, connecting with the Quran and being ambassadors of good in our society.

The most important and crucial aspect of change we need to make is regarding our mindset and way of thinking. I want to take you back to one of the most traumatic incidents in the life of the Prophet (saw), the slander against Aishah (ra). After Allah revealed verses establishing her innocence, He said about the incident in Surah Noor, "Think it not to be an evil to you: on the contrary, it is good for you." (Al-Quran 24:11) This verse highlights the exact paradigm through which we must view anything and everything that happens in our lives; it will be positive in the long run, and it will bring more good in reward than bad so long as we have the right attitude towards it. Once we begin to view problems such as negative campaign tactics and stereotypes through this lens, and understand that it is just a test, issues that once loomed before us like monsters now appear insignificant and trivial. Muslims in the USA have also have developed a habit of self-pity and exaggeration, as we hear phrases like "We are living in the worst of times" or,

"America is the worst place for Muslims," while in actuality we are not suffering any severe problems or trauma. Look at the Jews in the Holocaust. Look at the Japanese and African Americans right here not too long ago. Look at the oppressed Muslims in Syria, Palestine, East Turkistan and Burma, where they are scrutinized and even killed for their religious beliefs. We need to realize that the American constitution is one of the most equitable and impartial constitutions and it gives more rights to its citizens than most other countries, especially Muslim ones. Although we may not feel comfortable or secure living in this country, the fact of the matter is that we can freely practice our religion under the law, and we need to be extremely grateful for that by utilizing our resources wisely and not complaining.

The Quran is a rope connecting us with Allah, and by leaving that rope, we lose our connection with Allah. However, in today's charged environment, it seems that we have lost this valuable and crucial connection that we need to revive. The Quran gives us both hope and fear because as we read about the happiness and bliss that the believers will be surrounded in, our spirit and faith are boosted. We also read about the severe punishment that the disbelievers will undergo, and it is as if we can see them in front of our eyes. But we also need to read about the suffering that prophets and believers before us faced, and understand that life is not as going to be as easy as we would like. Allah says in the Quran, "Or did you think that you will enter Paradise without such (trials) as came to those who passed away before you? They were afflicted with severe poverty and ailments and were so shaken…" (Al-Quran 2:214) Allah is telling us in simple terms that if we want to reach the top, life is not always going to go our way. We are going to hit obstacles, and we need to work through them with the miracle of the Quran. Hope and fear; they create a balance between life's challenges. However, in order for us to truly benefit from the Quran, we need to understand it. Before Allah revealed verses prohibiting alcohol, he said, "Oh you who believe! Do not approach the prayer when you are in a drunken state until you know [the meaning] of what you utter..." (Al-Quran 4:43) Allah did not want them to pray until they understood the Quran. In Salah today, however, we are facing the same problem! Understanding Allah's words is what gives us the hope to push through difficulties, and it gives us the fear to keep away from actions that displease Allah, and hope in Allah and fear in him both raise the level of faith in our hearts.

One of the great blessings that Allah gave our Prophet Isa (as) is mentioned in Surah Maryam where He says, "And He has made me blessed wherever I am" (Surah Al-Quran 19:31) The scholars of Tafsir have said that this alludes to his consistent enjoining of good and forbidding of evil. Indeed, we see that some of the most praised and respected individuals in recent history such as Mahatma Ghandi and Mother Teresa were known for simply doing good wherever they were. The Prophet (saw) said in the well-known Hadith, "Be prompt in doing good deeds (before you are overtaken) by turbulence which would be like a part of the dark night. During (that stormy period) a man would be a Muslim in the morning and an unbeliever in the evening or he would be a believer in the evening and an unbeliever in the morning, and would sell his faith for worldly goods." (Muslim, Book #1, Hadith #220) Doing good is essentially a shield from the trials we face, as the Prophet (saw) warned us. These trials come like a stormy night, where it is too dark for one to differentiate between good and evil or the correct path to choose, except one who has prepared himself for it. Doing righteous deeds, whether big or small, keep the flame of faith strong and firm, and we cannot deny the genuine sense of happiness and contentment that comes with them. At the end of the Hadith, The Prophet (saw) says that an individual's faith will be so tempestuous and turbulent that it will flip in one day, and he will sell it for worldly goods, meaning that a student that is bullied because of his or her religion, for example, may leave parts of it just to fit in, or a person looking for a job may leave their religion behind just for a higher salary or a better position. The Prophet (saw) knew that this day would come and warned us against it. Anytime Allah mentions the believers in the Quran, he pairs it with righteous actions, indicating that belief must be followed through with action, and without righteous deeds we are helpless in this temporary and diminutive world as well as the hereafter. Doing good is also a great form of Da'wah, as good actions and elevated manners can call a person to the religion of Islam, by the will of Allah, better than anything else can.

A believer with strong faith is one who will truly be successful both in this life and the next. While it may seem difficult, keeping the flame of faith strong can be done in three main steps: Firstly, we must alter our way of thinking, and understand that many people have suffered far worse than us. Next, we must reconnect ourselves with the Quran, and try to understand its message. Lastly, we must represent Islam through good and righteous deeds, as actions speak louder than words. In closing, we should never forget or undermine the power of dua. We know from the prophetic tradition that only dua has the power to change the divine decree and that dua is the essence of worship. We make dua to Allah with the great dua that the Prophet (saw) used to say frequently, "O Controller of the hearts, make my heart steadfast in your religion." (Riyad As-Saliheen, Book, #17, Hadith #1489)

References:
1. Al-Quran, Surah #2 Ayah #214
2. Al-Quran, Surah #4 Ayah #43
3. Al-Quran, Surah #24 Ayah #11
4. Al-Quran, Surah #57 Ayah #28
5. Riyad As-Saliheen, Book #17, Hadith #1489
6. Sahih Muslim, Book #1, Hadith #220

SECOND PLACE
Nazifa Mahmud, College Park, Md.
Al-Huda School

How to Keep the flame of faith alive?

Amidst fear of attacks, agitation, trauma, and agony, it is exasperating to stay within the right path and not go astray. Suicides, assassinations, bombings, and radicalism are some of the prevalent terms to trace the world we live in these days. Violence is a disease which has not been cured by us and it is contagious to a point that it has been going on for centuries. Picture the lives of the Palestinians who lost the roof from above their heads, the evacuation of many Syrians, the carnage of innocent people, and all the other nightmares that the world has immersed itself in. These days, it is unfeasible to not have a story construed with delinquencies or casualties on the news. All these heart throbbing incidents have made many of us lose the norms of good behavior, and subsequently, led us to despair. As Muslim believers, it is pivotal for us to keep the leap of our faith resilient to cope with all the negativities confined within us. Being persistent in our faith can unleash the door of darkness to a ray of sunshine.

The list of casualties that surround the Muslim ummah can go on and on, but we must not be consumed by these negative events and instead learn to combat them with patience, good companions, and following the words of the Quran and the ways of the Prophet Muhammad (saw). First and foremost, you must be patient when you face hardships. Allah says in the Quran 11:49 "So be patient; indeed, the [best] outcome is for the righteous."(1) Patience helps you deal with your problems by making you more aware of your surroundings and avoid irritability.

Keeping your faith strong can be done very easily by following the footsteps of Prophet Muhammad (saw). Prophet Muhammad (saw) faced hardships more than anyone will ever face in this world, and Allah sent him as a role model of what every human should do when others try to humiliate, torture or even kill them. No one can ever be as good as the Prophet (saw), however, by even staying close to how he dealt with some situations that would get in the way of his belief, we can achieve more faith in our hearts. For example, staying silent when people threaten or curse you, doing the acts that Allah (swt) has commanded you to do, hide or run away from life threatening situations. One example of how the Prophet (saw) dealt with his problems was when people during the time of Jahilliyyah tried to kill the Prophet (saw), he (saw) migrated from his hometown of Mecca to Medina, leaving all his belongings and family behind.(2) This was a time of distress for the Prophet that he dealt with patience by hiding out to avoid fighting, instead of conspiring against the enemies. This teaches us that it's important to stay away from fighting when terrible times come, and just to be silent.

Many distractions nowadays such as television shows and music videos are very hard to stay away from. It is very easy for Shaytan to make us stray away from the right path. However, we should always remember when you start losing your faith, read the quran and follow it's guidance.(4) The quran has all the solutions to your problems and the only thing missing from your problems and their solutions is you taking the time to read over the precious words of Allah (swt).

Sometimes disbelievers can effect our hearts in a way that makes us question our religion. The best way to overcome this kind of situation is to search for answers. Remember that Allah has allowed us Muslims to ask questions to learn more, unlike any other religion there is. In most cases, questioning another religion is seen as a sinful deed. Instead of giving up and following ignorant people that try to derive you from your religion, we should be searching the web and defending our own religion. Nowadays, finding scholarly opinions and religious information can be found very easily just by the click of a button.

Another way to avoid getting caught in situations that make you question your religion is to avoid hanging out with people that might have a bad influence on you. The Prophet (saw) said, "A person is upon the religion of his close friend, so beware whom you befriend." [Abu Daawood and At-Tirmithi] (3)When you are around people that commit sinful acts, they will most likely convince you do the things they do and you may eventually lose your ability to distinguish between right and wrong. You may even become the victim of peer pressure which can harm your faith. However, a good friend will always help you do the right things. For instance, being amongst faithful people can also make your faith stronger. You can always learn from each other and help each other in times of hardship, such as moments that may make you leave your religion. The Prophet (saw) was reportedly asked: "Which of our companions are best?" He replied: "One whose appearance reminds you of God, and whose speech increases you in knowledge, and whose actions remind you of the hereafter."(3)

If you don't have good friends, and you are unable to find solutions to your problems, you can always rely on Allah for help when you think you might be digressing away from your faith. "And when My slaves ask you (O Muhammad (saw)) concerning Me, then (answer them), I am indeed near (to them by My Knowledge). I respond to the invocations of the supplicant when he calls on Me (without any mediator or intercessor). So let them obey Me and believe in Me, so that they may be led aright" [Al-Quran, 2:186] (1) This ayah shows the best way to keep our faiths strong: it is to ask Allah for help and he will surely answer your duas. Whenever you are trying to get out of a situation that weakens your faith, you need to make dua to Allah. Allah has asked us to ask him for help several times in the Quran and the Prophet (saw) also mentions getting closer to Allah by making dua. Allah said that he loves when his slaves ask for His help, thus the more you ask Allah, the better. You can ask Allah for anything, starting from the forgiveness for a great sin to a good test grade on your final.

If you are losing hope and your duas aren't getting accepted, you should ask yourself 'Are you doing your part to make your faith stronger?' Making dua does not guarantee that they will be answered, rather, you need to get involved and put your faith into action. By practicing the religion, you will be able to think and feel your faith and make it stronger. To get involved, you can do simple things such as spending more time with your family, volunteer in your community, or join a organization that you might think would help you make a positive difference in your life and the lives of others.

To make faith stronger in your heart you need to take the chances that you heart wants you to take. You need to be prepared to act against your desires and stand with what you know is best for you. You need to let your heart be filled with faith and you need to suck out even the smallest amount of evil that tempts you to do wrong.

'Take what is given freely, enjoin what is good, and turn away from the ignorant.' (1) (Al-Quran 7:199)

'And if an evil suggestion comes to you from Satan, then seek refuge in Allah . Indeed, He is Hearing and Knowing.' (1) (Al-Quran 7:200)

References:
1. Quran.com
2. http://www.beliefnet.com/columnists/ everydayinspiration/2013/08/your-faith- strong-in- tough-times. html#XWXiFsQ1HULkV5o3.99
3. https://www.quora.com/What-are-some-stories-of-the-sadness-and-suffering-endured-by-our-prophet-peace-be-upon-him-during-the-time-of-prophet-hood
4. http://hadithoftheday.com/6-tips-to-remain-steadfast-in-faith/

THIRD PLACE
Daiyan Musabbir, College Park, Md.
Al Huda School

"It is understood that faith is affirmation and not merely belief. Affirmation includes the words of the heart, which is belief, and the actions of the heart, which is compliance." This is how Ibn Taymiyyah (ra) defined faith. True faith, then, must manifest itself in the heart as sincerity, on the tongue as affirmation, and on the limbs as action. As Muslims living in a predominantly non-Muslim country, it is expected that we will face obstacles meant to challenge and extinguish our faith. We find it difficult to proudly identify as Muslims because of our innate fear of being categorized as the "other". The Muslim Ummah has become accustomed to conforming to the societal norms, and this has become especially apparent in the Muslim Youth. So how do we, as youth, fight this ceaseless battle to keep our faith strong under the negative and adverse conditions we live in? The problem is a complex one, that has afflicted the hearts, minds, and the bodies of the believers. The only successful method of action is following the solution that is delineated in the Quran and Sunnah, which is the sole way we will keep the faith raging in the hearts of the believers and against the challenges we are faced with daily.

Before searching for a solution, we must understand the problem that we are plagued with. Why is it so difficult to perform actions that Allah has commanded us to perform? We know it is our duty and obligation as Muslims, yet, we are hesitant and sometimes even fearful to follow his commands. This is a disease of the heart, and it has crept into many believers' hearts today. Instead of having Taqwa, fear, of Allah and having complete Tawakkul, or trust in Him, we are more fearful of what people will say about us or how they perceive us. We have become so accustomed to pleasing our peers and fearing their judgement that we have forgotten who we are made to please and fear. Brothers are shaving their beards, saying it bothers them. This is utterly disrespectful to Allah(Swt) and many of the believers today have turned serious matters into things they deem measly. The beard is Fard (obligatory) upon the man, so the narrative that it is fine to shave your beard shows the lack of faith in our own community. Furthermore, sisters are taking their hijabs off because of a odd look they got or commentary made by a stranger. Allah (Swt) says: "O Prophet Enjoin your wives, your daughters, and the wives of believers to draw their cloaks over them [when they go out]. That is more proper, so that they may be distinguished and not be harassed. Surely, God is the most forgiving and merciful. (Al-Quran, 33:59) Our ummah will never be able to hold onto the flame of faith in our hearts or fight any challenges we face until we change what inside us. The change starts from within. We need to stop examining the actions of our body without even beginning to scrutinize the condition of our hearts. Imam al-Sadiq (as) has said: "The heart possesses two ears, the spirit of belief slowly invites him towards righteous deeds, while the Satan slowly invites him towards evil deeds. Therefore, whoever becomes victorious in this struggle takes over heart's control." It is clear that the fight we must first overcome is the one that is internal, before we have the ability to fight any negativity externally.

Once we have identified the problem within ourselves, this is when we can begin to address and overcome the challenges we encounter externally. Allah (swt) has illustrated a clear step-by-step guide for us to follow to help us with this problem. He says:

> "And who is better in speech than he who [says: "My Lord is Allah" and then stands firm and] invites [men] to Allah's and does righteous deeds and says: "I am one of the Muslims." The good deed and the evil deed cannot be equal. Repel [the evil] with one which is better; then verily he between whom and you there was enmity [will become] as though he was a closed friend.(Al-Quran, 41:33-34)

In these ayaat, Allah (swt) explains to us clearly what we must do in order to overcome these hardships. The verse illustrates the best way to handle ignorance and hate, through speech, and the best speech is calling to Allah.

The ayaat states the best of words is not the most scholarly and the most melodious, rather it is the Call to people to embrace faith. This is the first step that should be taken against those who are hateful against our deen. The people that will keep their faith raging in their hearts are those who call people to embrace true faith. Their words and deeds are the best.

Secondly, one calling people to embrace faith must do righteous good deeds so that his words impress the audience and his actions reinforce his words. If a person is spewing hateful comments and going on tirades against your deen, it is your duty as a Muslim to show them what is right not only by your words, but also by what you do.

Lastly, a person must take pride in their Muslim faith and identity. If you are not able to proudly say "I am a Muslim", how will we ever change what people think or say about Muslims. The ability to respect and cherish our own identities is an essential aspect in fighting these obstacles of hate and negativity that we face.

When we understand that we are not required to conform to society, that is when our faith will be at its strongest. When we as an Ummah stop seeking acceptance and acknowledgment from this immoral society that we are in, that is when we will not be distraught by this negativity and hate that we face. That is when our faith will not falter for any reason, because we understand that we are here on this Earth for a short time, and our duty is to please and worship Allah. These challenges are tests from Allah to see if our faith is steadfast, and the answers to His test have been given to us in the Quran. If we can get to this point of complete faith as an Ummah, then the flame of faith in the hearts of the believers will never be extinguished.

References:
1. "Ramadan - Rules of Fasting the Blessed Month." Alsunna.org - Islamic information per Qur'an and Alsunna., www.alsunna.org/Proofs-on-the-obligations-of-Hijab-Veil.html.
2. "The Heart in Quran." Al-Islam.org, www.al-islam.org/self-building-ayatullah-ibrahim-amini/heart-quran.
3. "The definition of faith in Islam." Faith in Allah, 16 Aug. 2015, abuaminaelias.com/the-definition-of-faith-in-islam/.

2019

Civility, Ethics, and Morality

Essay Panel Contest
2019

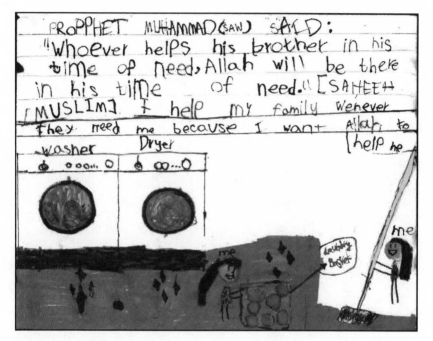

This poster was submitted by Ayesha Mahmood in the Level 1 competition.

ELEMENTARY SCHOOL, LEVEL 1
Grades 1 & 2

Civility, Ethics, and Morality

Which moral values have I learned from my religion and how do I uphold these in my interaction with friends and family?

FIRST PLACE
Merium Ahmad, Lanham, Md.
Homeschool

Bismillah
November 19, 2018
Dear Jenna,

Assalamualaykom. How are you?

I hope you like my present. I was at the store and I saw a bag. I asked Mom if I could buy it. She said, "Yes".

Then I asked my mom if I could get one for you too, and she said, "Yes." She said this is how Prophet Muhammad (saw) told us to be. He (saw) said,

"لَا يُؤْمِنُ أَحَدُكُمْ حَتَّى يُحِبَّ لِأَخِيهِ مَا يُحِبُّ لِنَفْسِهِ" .

(Bukhari and Muslim)

This means we should love for others what we love for ourselves and treat others like we want to be treated. So we should speak in a nice way not like a donkey braying. We should not hit anyone even if they hit us. When we play, we should share. I should not say no if my sister asks to borrow my jewelry. When we give candy we give the same to them not the ones that we do not like and keep the good ones. This is how we follow the hadith.

That's why I got you the bag I liked and I hope you like it too!

Love,
Merium

SECOND PLACE
Alisha Mia, Columbia, Md.
Maryum Islamic Center

Dear Manha,

Assalamu alaikum warahmatullah. I like to share with you about a good Muslim. I really want to be a good Muslim. My religion (Islam) taught me that to be a good Muslim, I have to follow Allah's rules and His Messenger Muhammad (saw). I also need to be kind to His creations especially human being. Surah Maun taught me that a good Muslim must not push away orphans and hungry people; she is focus on her prayers; she doesn't do any good deed to show off but to please Allah; she is always happy to help other people.

I am happy to pray with my mom and dad at home. Prophet Muhammad (saw) thought us smiling at a person is a good deed. I like to smile at my family members and others. I am nice to my friends and family and eager to help them whenever I can. I try to use polite words such as "thank you", "sorry" and "excuse me". I help my parents to keep our house clean.

I also try to be nice to animals and insects. I know that the beautiful surroundings are created by Allah. I learnt from a Hadith not to tear down a leaf or tree branch unnecessarily.
A good Muslim is also a caring person. She cares about her neighbors and our environment. She likes to keep our environment clean and beautiful.

A good Muslim pleases Allah by worshiping Him and respecting other. I know that to remain a good Muslim, I need to follow Allah and His Messenger Muhammad (saw) and be kind to His creations. A good Muslim is a valuable person for our society.

Sincerely,
Alisha

THIRD PLACE
Sumayyah Ahmed, Herndon, Va.
Al Minar Academy

Dear Sarah,

السَّلامُ عَلَيْكُمْ!!

How are you?! How was your winter break? I am joining an EPC competition for my winter break and while I'm doing it I learned some amazing, cool stuff. It is about morality. I learned in Islam not to eat pork, not to drink alcohol and to wear a hijab so it can cover my hair. I also learned to not do bad, to do good and to be a good Muslim. Allah (swt) created us to worship him, not just for fun. He wanted to test us in the world, that's why. If we don't listen to Allah (swt), then he will get sad. And we don't want Allah (swt) to be sad. Allah (swt) has given me a lot of stuff that helps us like food, drinks, and lots of other stuff like that. So we should be grateful to Allah (swt) and also listen to him. Allah (swt) takes away a lot of people so quick, even in prayer. Let me tell you a story about a man. There was a muslim who use to drink alcohol and never used to pray. Another muslim man was walking to the masjid and he saw the man drinking alcohol. He said to him, "Stop drinking. Come to the masjid." The man said, "Fine!" When they went to the masjid, everyone started bullying the man who drank alcohol. He prayed in a corner of the masjid. In sujood, the man who drank alcohol passed away. So even if you are bad, you must say sorry and mean it, then Allah (swt) will forgive you.

I'll tell you another story. Adam (as) didn't obey Allah (Awt). He ate from a tree that Allah (swt) said not to. But he said, "Sorry" and Allah forgave him. Shaytan got really proud and never said sorry. Now Shaytan is making people proud. It is haram to be proud. Allah (swt) can even take peoples' tongues away. Shaytan made someone named Al Ghazali really proud. Al Ghazali was a scholar who used to give so many lectures in front of thousands of people.

One day, Allah (swt) made Al Ghazali lost his tongue. Al Ghazali was a really good man so he said, "I'm going to hajj ." But he was not only going to hajj, he was also going somewhere else. For ten years, he lived as a sweeper in a masjid where nobody knew him. He got his voice back and was not proud anymore. So he went back to his home. Later, he was close to his death.

When people die we should say inna lillahi wa inna ilaihi raji'un, meaning, "We are from Allah (swt) and to Him we will return." You should say that for a couple of minutes. Or if you want you could do it for an hour. So when we return to him, He should be pleased with us. If we are moral, that means do the right things, if we say sorry when we do wrong like Adam (as), and if we fix our behavior like Al Ghazali, then we will go to Jannah and have a good life.

Give my Salams to your Mom and Dad,
I really hope you have the best time!
Assalamu alaikum Sarah!!!

                              Love,
                              Sumayyah

Essay Panel Contest
2019

This poster was submitted by Yusuf Mehmood in the Level 2 competition.

ELEMENTARY SCHOOL, LEVEL 2
Grades 3 & 4

Civility, Ethics, and Morality

Identify something you learned about the moral values in Islam at your home and outside as a Muslim. What do you do to maintain your moral values when interacting with your friends and family members? What do you do to uphold your moral values? Is it difficult to keep up the moral values? How does your moral values help build your identity?

FIRST PLACE
Yusuf Mehmood, Glenelg, Md.
MCC Weekend School and Bushy Park Elementary School

Choo choo! Choo choo! Welcome aboard the good character train. Buckle their seat belts, we are in for a ride! Today you will be learning about 3 important moral values that will help you to become a better Muslim. The 3 cabins I will be discussing are courage, kindness and truthfulness. Let's begin the tour!

Our first cabin is called courage. As a Muslim boy, it is important for me to have courage and strength when it comes to my identity. People ask me a lot of questions about Islam at school. Ever since KG my parents have doing presentations on Eid and Ramadan. It takes a lot of courage to be unique. I practice courage at home when I make a mistake, I need to have courage to accept my faults. I have courage to stand up for what is right. It can be hard to have courage to speak up sometimes but my mom teaches me everyday to be confident of my identity.

We are now moving on to the our second cabin called kindness. I learned a hadith in Sunday school about kindness: Aisha (ra) stated that Rasul (saw) said: "O Aisha, Allah is kind and He loves kindness in all matters" (Bukhari) (1). After I heard this hadith, I started thinking about how I try my best to be kind at home. I help my mother with chores around the house. I also show kindness at school by being helpful and caring. I am part of a group called Muslim Scouts of Maryland, here I have learned a lot about kindness. I make lunches for the homeless and visit the elderly. Kindness is a very easy moral character to follow. I am a nice and gentle person so it is in my identity to be kind.

The last cabin we will visit today is called truthfulness. In Surah Tawbah Allah says: "O you who have believed, fear Allah and be with those who are true." (1) (Muslim, Book#39 Hadith#11) It is important to tell the truth and it is important to have truthful friends. Lying at home or at school will only get you in deeper trouble. Rasul (saw) was known as As-Sadiq and Al-Ameen, I want to be just like him.

I went on umrah this year and went to Masjid An-Nabi. I was very inspired this trip to be a good person. I want the moral values taught by Rasul (saw) to become part of my personality. Our beloved Prophet (saw) was the best of mankind. He (saw) said: "The best of people are those with the most excellent character." (3) The Prophet Muhammad (saw) is my role model. I hope you enjoyed being on the good character train with me. I think if you stay on this train, your moral values will be perfect in no time. Choo Choo!

References:
1. Sahih Muslim
2. Surah Tawbah: Ayah 119
3. Sahih Tabarani

SECOND PLACE
Hafsa Khan, College Park, Md.
Al Huda School

What are moral values? Being generous, honest, trustworthy, loyal, just, and helpful are all examples of moral values. Which person comes to your mind who has all of these qualities and more? Yes, the Prophet Muhammad (saw)! I have learned from the example of the Prophet (saw) and our religion Islam, that I must always have the best morals when interacting with my friends, family, and community members.

One moral value that I try to practice is being generous. I recently took a field trip with my class to New York and I bought two cool souvenir pens. I really wanted both pens for myself but I started thinking about my brother's pen collection and how he would really love a pen from New York City . I struggled in my mind because I wanted both pens but I thought about the hadith of the Prophet (saw) that none of you truly believes until you love for your brother what you love for yourself. I gave my brother one of the pens to earn Allah swt's pleasure and hoped that if I was generous to him, next time he might be generous with me.

Another moral value that I have learned is being trustworthy. Can others trust us and not worry that we will do or say something to hurt them? It is very important that we are trustworthy and don't lie so that others can feel comfortable telling us important information or having us look after their belongings. In Surah An-Nahl, verse 91, Allah (swt) forbids Muslims to break their promises after they have confirmed them. How would we feel if we told our friend a secret and they went and told others, or how would our teacher feel if we asked to go to the bathroom and instead we meet our friends and hang out in the hallway?

Islam also teaches us to be just which means to be fair. In our school, I am part of Dar Al Farooq, or the house of justice. Did you know that the nickname of Omar ibn Al Khattab was Al Farooq because he was a fair leader.   He never made anyone become Muslim and he made sure everyone was treated fairly. Are we fair when playing a game with our friends or family? Are we fair when our parents tell us to share a candy bar with our siblings or do we break it so that we get the biggest piece? In Surah Nahl, ayah 90, Allah swt orders justice and good conduct.

It is very important that we uphold moral values like the Prophet Muhammad (saw) so that we can live a good life, please Allah swt and earn jannah. Even though it might be difficult, we know that the Prophet saw said, "Indeed the most perfect among the believers is of the best of morals." Let's do our best to be of those who are the best in the sight of Allah (swt)!

References:
1. Islamicity.org. (2019) Umar ibn al Khattab among the most influential people in history. Retrieved from https://www.islamicity.org/4031/umar-ibn-al-khattab-among-the-most-influential-people-in-history/
2. Hilālī, T. A., Khan, M. M., & Bukhārī, M. I. (2010). Interpretation of the meanings of the noble Quran in the English language:. Darussalam.

THIRD PLACE
Mustafaa Ahmed, College Park, Md.
M&M Learning Center

Everyday, we are faced with situations where we have to think about how our actions will hurt or help us and others around us. Knowing what is right and wrong is what morality is. Alhamdulillah, I am a Muslim. Being a Muslim means that you have to follow certain rules in your daily life. Allah (swt) teaches us these rules in the Quran, so that we do not have to guess what is right and wrong. We also have the example of the Prophet Muhammad (saw). For me, my daily life is full of reminders on how to live as a good Muslim. I have a big family, so certain moral lessons come up everyday. Lessons on honesty, kindness, being fair, being happy with what Allah has given me, not to be jealous or greedy and avoiding backbiting are some of the things my parents have to remind me about constantly. It is not easy living with many people at home and even when going to school, I have to be with people from so many backgrounds, without sometimes falling into the trap of doing something I should not be doing. For instance, it can be easy to lie about something to avoid getting into trouble. I also have to watch out for backbiting about people in my class when I talk with my siblings. In school, it can be easy to cheat on a test if I am stuck on an answer or to be unkind to someone who is also being mean to me. These are challenges that I face every day.

There are many ways in which I try to do the better thing in a situation. The first thing is that I am trying to pray all of my 5 daily prayers on time. At home we usually pray as a family but sometimes we don't so that is when I need to remind myself to pray. Secondly, my parents are constantly sharing stories with us about how the Prophet Muhammad (saw) was the best in moral character and that we all need to strive to be like him. Allah (swt) says in Surah Al-Qalam, Ayah 4: "Indeed, you are of a great moral character" talking about the Prophet Muhammad (saw). My parents also provide us with books that teach good lessons. I love the Noor Kids series. They have many stories about how not to lie, backbite or be unkind. I think these books really helped me because the characters are young and I can relate to them. They teach me to be fair with my siblings when we are playing and to not get them in trouble just to save myself. When I am in school, my parents remind me to be very respectful to my teachers and if someone says or does something I do not like, then to nicely ask them to stop. They tell me that I cannot control what others do to me but I can control what I do, so I should say Bismillah and then control my anger. This will make Allah happy with me in sha Allah.

Trying to have good moral character and doing the right thing is not easy, especially if others around us don't care about how they act. However, being a good Muslim means to always strive to please Allah, so if I remember this all of the time, I can always try very hard to do the right thing, in sha Allah. In a hadith by Abu Darda, the Prophet (saw) said, On the Day of Reckoning, the most weighty item in the Scales of Deeds will be good manners".

I hope I can always have good manners so that I can go to Jannah, in sha Allah. These are some ways I practice morality in Islam.

References:
1. The Holy Quran
2. http://www.youngmuslimdigest.com/hadith/05/2012/morals-and-manners-in-islam/

Essay Panel Contest
2019

This poster was submitted by Saadiq Ahmed in the Level 3 competition.

MIDDLE SCHOOL, LEVEL 3
Grades 5 & 6

Civility, Ethics, and Morality

It's important to differentiate between the nature of morality in Islam and the morality without Islam – particularly in an age where good and evil are often looked at as relative concepts. Discuss what the morality in Islam means to you, what does it demand from you, why you should maintain it, and what is the consequence for not striving to attain moral values. Tell us about how you face the challenges in keeping up with your morality in your everyday interactions, and how you can confront immoral undertakings with your own words and actions as a Muslim.

FIRST PLACE
AbdurRahman Ali, Gaithersburg, Md.
Homeschool

One day, my parents went to a lecture by Imam Zaid Shakir. While he was giving the lecture, the topic of waking up for Fajr came up. He gave a solution on how to wake up. He said, "When you are feeling lazy, tell Satan, 'Hey Mr. Iblis, I'm going to wake up!' and say 'TANTANAN!!' ", and get out of bed quickly before you change your mind. We struggle with that all the time. Sometimes it is hard to choose from something that is morally correct and something that is bad, but fun.

Our morality comes from Allah and the Quran. The definition of morality is, something that is "relating to or concerned with the principles or rules of right conduct or the distinction between right and wrong; ethical." ("moral", dictionary.com) Allah created us, so He knows what is best for us. This is why we get our morality from our deen. An example of that is that of a car. The person who made the car knows what is best for the car. Let's say that the manual says to get an oil change after three thousand miles, but you want to get it after five thousand miles. What would happen to the car? It might work for some time, but it would break down soon. But it is just a car. What if you do that with yourself? If you don't listen to Allah's message, your body and soul wouldn't be healthy and you would eventually go to hellfire. You wouldn't like that. Therefore, we should follow Allah's commands so that we will lead a healthy life and go to paradise. Allah guides us in both our worship to him and our interaction with others-ibadat and muamalat and we must strive to uphold our morality in both aspects.

To have good moral character means to be a good person. Examples of a good moral character are justice, which means to be fair; truthfulness, which means telling the truth; kindness, which means to be compassionate, and generosity which means to be very giving. Sometimes, you have to choose between something good and something fun that is bad. An example of that is missing prayer to watch a soccer game or going to a friends house when you could have been memorizing Quran. We face these decisions every day.

It starts with Fajr. It takes a lot of energy to get out of your nice, cozy bed to pray Fajr. I struggle with it almost every day. But there are ways that I have learned. Not waking up for Fajr is not an option. One way to wake up is to recognize Satan and to take him as an enemy. Allah says in the Quran in Surah Fatir, ayah 6 "Indeed, Satan is an enemy to you; so take him as an enemy. He only invites his party to be among the companions of the Blaze." (Al-Quran, 36:60)

Another way to make sure you do something good when it is difficult to do so, is to give yourself consequences and rewards to encourage yourself. Let's go back to the example of Fajr. A way to encourage yourself is if you pray Fajr for one week on time, you eat one candy and if you don't wake up on time, you don't get to eat candy the next time you pray for a week.

In our daily lives, we deal not only with the deen but also with people and face the same challenges. If you are in public school and you have friends that bully others, you should tell them to stop bullying people. If they don't stop, ditch them and find better people to hang out with. The Prophet Muhammed (saw) said "Whosoever of you sees an evil, let him change it with his hand; and if he is not able to do so, then [let him change it] with his tongue; and if he is not able to do so, then with his heart – and that is the weakest of faith." [40 Hadith Nawawi, 34, sunnah.com]

People nowadays are not very good, and they choose what is fun over what is morally correct. We should all be morally correct in what we do, and we should recognize Satan and make sure we don't listen to what he says. We should all listen to the Quran and follow it. My principle and my way to deal with it is to just say, "TANTANAN!".

References:
1. Sunnah.com
2. Dictionary.com
3. Quran.com

SECOND PLACE
Ruwad Islam, College Park, Md.
Al Huda School

Everyday follows a very similar routine. I wake up in the morning, go to school, play with my sister when I come back home, do my homework, help my mom with chores, and finally eat and sleep. I am a student. I am a brother. I am a son. But above all, I am Muslim. Being Muslim means that I try my best to follow the moral characters in Islam. These moral characters include being patient, generous, courageous, truthful, and more. Nawas Ibn Sam'an reported that the Prophet of Allah, peace be upon him, was asked about doing good and evil. He replied, "Doing good is having good manners. Doing evil is what troubles you inside and what you would not like others to know about (Islamicity, 2018)." I like to live my day according to this hadith, by doing things that will please Allah (swt) and avoiding things that will get me into trouble, both in this life and the next.

Patience is a very important quality, but it is difficult to obtain. Uthman is a Sahabi who demonstrated great patience. He was a patient man who was ready to make sacrifices at any time in the name of Islam. I enjoy playing soccer and I have to make a lot of decisions while playing it. So, similar to Uthman, I have to be patient by not hogging the ball and I make sacrifices by passing the ball to other players whenever I can even if I feel like I can score. In surah Luqman it says "O my son, establish prayer, enjoin what is right, forbid what is wrong, and be patient over what befalls you. Indeed, that is of the matters determination."(Al-Quran 31:17)

Whenever I win the soccer games, I make sure not to brag too much about it, because I know it will make the other team sad. I do this because I understand the feelings of others and try not to hurt them.

Having good character means having good noticeable traits. How do I connect moral character with everyday life? I listen and help my elders because the Prophet (saw) told us to do so. I have a younger sibling, and I help her with her homework. I try not to lie so people will trust me. I help my mother in the kitchen when she needs assistance. I share my food with my friends when they ask me. I ignore people when they curse at me. All Muslims should have good moral character, so the non-Muslims will know that Muslims aren't bad. Morality in Islam demands people to be nice to everyone and be sincere, and you never know the true impact your good actions could have on a person.

Muslims should maintain a good moral character, so people won't think that they are bad. All of us deal with decisions of morality on a daily basis and the best thing to do is to follow what Allah and the prophet told us to do. Make good choices in life and avoid the bad ones. There are six good character traits mentioned in the Quran which are: purity/cleanliness, consuming halal food, walking modestly, speaking gently, being kind, and being hospitable (MuslimInc, n.d.). Cleanliness includes both physical and spiritual purity. To be spiritually pure means to not do any bad deeds. To be physically pure means to means to have good hygiene. To consume halal food means to eat everything halal and not haram, so that you can remain on the right path. To walk modestly means to walk in a humble way and not the arrogant way because walking in an arrogant way is the trait of shaytaan and it must be avoided. We should speak gently and not raise our voices or use foul language. To be hospitable means to make the guest happy while they stay at your house. We should make them feel comfortable. Some sahabas were really kind and generous even if they weren't wealthy. We must strive hard to develop these characteristics if we wish to be successful in this life and the hereafter.

When we are gardening, we need to make a hole in the soil and then put the seed inside. We need to water it, give it good soil, and sunlight if we want the plant to grow and give us fruits. Similarly, we can take care of ourselves by following the Quran and sunnah if we want to become a successful Muslim.

We can have good moral character in everyday life situations. We should try to always have good moral character because there are also consequences for those who do immoral actions. If we do immoral actions they will give us bad deeds which will lead us to jahannam. However, if we follow the right path then it will lead us to jannah. There are so many possible moral actions a person can do and follow. As a middle school student, my days typically follow the same routine. It might get boring at times, but nonetheless, I know that it is important to be patient when I don't like something, be kind to my parents and siblings, and follow the six character traits in my daily life so that I can be a good student, caring brother, loving son, and above all, obedient Muslim.

References:
1. Islamicity.org. (2018). 5 A hadith About Good Character - IslamiCity. [online] Available at: https://www.islamicity. org/12534/5-ahadith-about-good-character [Accessed 4 Jan. 2019].
2. MuslimInc. (n.d.). 6 Good character traits described in the Holy Quran. [online] Available at: http://musliminc.com/6-good-character-traits-described-in-the-holy-quran-14219 [Accessed 4 Jan. 2019].

THIRD PLACE
Neemat Mehedi, Springfield, Va.
Al-Qalam Academy

Morality in Islam

Is morality in Islam the same as morality without Islam? They may seem like they are the same idea, but in fact they are not. Morality without Islam is mostly about knowing the difference between right and wrong or good and bad in relation to each other and based on the laws of the country. One example is that everyone, including non-religious people, knows that they should not steal from someone else, because they can be punished by the law. Morality in Islam may be like that, but it is also connected to our beliefs and duties and defined by our religion.

What is the definition of morality in Islam? To be a good Muslim with morality, we need to follow the five pillars of Islam: the Shahada, Salah, Zakat, Sawm and Hajj. And we also need to be kind to others, forgiving, respectful, and giving, just like our Prophet Muhammad (saw) was.

Morality is mentioned in so many surahs of the Quran. One example is in Surah Al-Hujurat, ayah number 11: "O you who believe! Let not some men among you laugh at others: it may be that the (latter) are better than the (former): nor let some women laugh at others: it may be that the (latter) is better than the (former): nor defame nor be sarcastic to each other, nor call each other by offensive nicknames: ill-seeming is a name connoting wickedness, (to be used of one) after he has believed: and those who don't desist are (indeed) doing wrong." This ayah is about being good to others and that is part of morality.

Why do we maintain morality? Let's think about it. Isn't morality a huge part in Islam? A huge part in being human? Without morality, your heart will be nothing, frozen even. What made you human is gone. That's why, personally, I think maintaining morality is important. Without it, your heart will just be empty of any emotions and it will become easier to make bad decisions. The consequences for not having morality are to be humiliated before Allah in the Day of Judgment. Immoral people, if they are not forgiven, will dwell in Jahannam.

What does it mean to have good moral character? Kindness, forgiveness, respect, charity, honesty, trustworthiness and modesty are all associated with having good moral character. It was narrated by Abu Hurayrah that the Prophet (saw) said: "There is no day on which the people get up but two angels come down and one of them says, `O Allah, give in compensation to the one who spends (in charity). `And the other says, `O Allah, destroy the one who withholds. `" (Al Bukhaari, 1374; Muslim, 1010).

Everyone has to deal with decisions of morality on a daily basis. At school, you see a lot of things you don't think is right. You see people shunning other people because they think they are "weird." Avoiding them in classes, not sitting with them in lunch and even gossiping about them. The thing is that those people who are being shunned feel hurt and start thinking that there is something wrong with them even though there is not. It is morally wrong to make others feel bad about them and exclude them from your group. Sometimes kids don't understand that gossiping is wrong, and that it can lead to other immoral actions such as backbiting and bullying.

As a Muslim, we should reassure the kids getting bullied, sit with them at lunch, and be their friend. As for the kids who are bullying them, try to tell them that gossiping about someone is wrong. After all, in Islam we are all brothers and sisters. That is what I try to remember and do. But there are still challenges. Those people might start gossiping about you, push you around and hurt your feelings.

Despite these challenges, we should strive to attain moral values and maintain them. The important thing to remember is that Allah will help you overcome your challenges, so never forget Him. In conclusion, morality in Islam is very important, and you need it to be a good Muslim.

MIDDLE SCHOOL, LEVEL 4
Grades 7 & 8

Civility, Ethics, and Morality

It's important to differentiate between the nature of morality in Islam and the morality without Islam – particularly in an age where good and evil are often looked at as relative concepts. Discuss what the morality in Islam means to you, what does it demand from you, why you should maintain it, and what is the consequence for not striving to attain moral values. Tell us about how you face the challenges in keeping up with your morality in your everyday interactions, and how you can confront immoral undertakings with your own words and actions as a Muslim.

FIRST PLACE
Jinan Ahmad, Herndon, Va.
Al-Minar Homeschool Academy

When I was younger, I would always anticipate the part of the day when my teacher would begin the Seerah in Islamic studies. As she told us stories of the Prophet Muhammad (saw), I would sit at the edge of my seat, devouring every word. I noticed that I had grown in my love for the Prophet (saw) ever since we had started our Seerah class. I would try to act like him, as I followed his moral qualities the best I could. Now, looking back, I see learning and trying to behave like the Prophet has helped me so much as I grow older. I have noticed the most important things the youth should have in order to live a truly happy life, is to have a healthy educational childhood while practicing their own code of moral values, know how to deal with daily decisions of morality, and have a morally good character that benefits society as well.

As children brought up in the Muslim community, we are instilled with Islamic virtues and qualities. Little things taught to us by parents and teachers, such as holding the door for someone, saying salaam to your parents on a regular basis, and even just being cheerful, have large impacts on your life and the lives of those around you. Since our childhood is a precious period of our life, it is important that we practice good moral values and etiquette from our early years.

The Qur'an and Hadith serve as a primary source for moral values and ethics for the youth to learn from on their own. Both often describe in an emphatic manner instructing the Muslims to have a morally good character. Respecting one's parents and elders, helping the poor and needy, being kind to people and to animals, forgiving others, and being honest come as major virtues in Islamic concept and morality. Not only does reading the Quran and Hadith help with one's character, but they also help with becoming closer to Allah and his Messenger.

As a Muslim, to understand morality in Islam, one doesn't have to look far. The best example of good moral character is our Prophet Muhammad (saw), the best of mankind. Prophet Muhammad (saw) is the Messenger sent from Allah as a role model for all of humanity to follow. The morals of the Prophet were always so elevated and praiseworthy that Allah has regarded them as great in the Holy Qur'an; `And truly you (Muhammad) possess great morals' (68:4) Surah Al- Qalam. There is no greater role model to help us, the youth, stay on the straight path and make the right choices.

Every day kids and teens face decisions of morality, whether it be on the internet, school or even at home. You could face some bullies at school, get teased by your siblings at home, or be faced with coming across something inappropriate on the internet. There are many little tests in life that either take you away from the right path or bring you closer to it. For us, Muslims, it is important we face these problems with grace and humility. For example, if the class bully approaches you and starts verbally abusing you, it's best to turn to Allah for help and ignore the best you can. But if things get worse and the bully shows no intention of stopping, it is important you turn to an adult for help. Allah will help you as long as you help yourself the best you can. But since you faced this problem with dignity, in the future, you will not regret your actions.

With more trivial things, someone taking your credit or a sibling teasing you, it's best to just keep patience and tell your friend or sibling calmly, not to do it again. Such is the behavior of the Prophet (Saw), who has faced more animosity than anyone else. Having even small amounts of his qualities will only elevate you in life.

If a person has been raised with high moral standards, they will not only be benefiting themselves but society as well. These days it is very rare to find someone who is just good. We seem to question them because it seems so unusual to find a person who is good without anything to gain. That's why it is important for the Muslim youth to be taught these moral qualities so that society may look up to Muslims instead of down.

We, the Youth, must be a good example to those who come in the future, so that they may be proud to be Muslim, instead of trying to conceal it: so that they may be loved and admired instead of feared and hated. In order for the future to be like this, we, the Muslims, must educate our youth, enrich them with knowledge and understanding. Teach them to have good moral qualities and ethics. Most definitely read the Seerah to them. Only then will the future of our Muslim community, be in secure hands.

References:

1. https://en.wikipedia.org/wiki/Morality_in_Islam
2. http://www.arabnews.com/islam-perspective/news/641661
3. https://www.newmuslims.com/lessons/330/morals-of-prophet-muhammad-part-1/
4. https://www.newmuslims.com/lessons/329/morals-of-prophet-muhammad-part-2/

SECOND PLACE
Nabeel Chowdhury, Greenbelt, Md.
Al-Huda School

Morality in Islam circles around the basic tenets of our deen. But what is morality, and what does it mean to have good moral character? To be moral is to be able to distinguish between right and wrong in our daily actions. You should not be arrogant and show off when you are the only one who got full marks on a quiz in your class. You should not raise your voice or be angry, even when something or someone is bothering you. You should help a senior citizen when they are crossing the street. You should always respect the people around you, especially those who are older than you. The Islamic moral system stems from its primary creed of belief in

Allah as the Creator and Sustainer of the Universe. The underlying idea of Islamic morality is that of love for Allah and His creatures.

In Islam, it is important to have good moral character. In a hadith narrated by Abu Hurayrah, The Prophet (saw) says, "The best among you are those with the best manners, so long as they develop a sense of understanding". Backing up this hadith, Allah says in surah Ash Shu'ara," The Day when there will not benefit [anyone] wealth or children. But only one who comes to Allah with a sound heart." This hadith and the ayah says that we will not be considered the best people unless we have good manners and morals, and we are satisfied and grateful for what we have in our lives. We will not reach Jannah without these attributes. Therefore it is important to have a good moral character in Islam. It is a key component to enter the doors of Jannah. Furthermore, one should be morally upright in Islam because Allah will be happy with them and they will be a step closer to achieving Jannah.

Moral characteristics define who you are. It shows your personality either as a bad person or as a good person. Your first impression on someone can show who you are as a person, and can make or break your relationship with that person. It is best to have good morals so that people look up to you and respect you. Without good morals, you will not have anybody on your side when you need them the most. Morality in Islam demands continuous self-evaluation and correction to stay on and observe the commandments of Allah and follow the Quran. If you are not morally upright, it is as though you have committed a sin and Allah will not come to your aid when you are in need, and He will make it harder for you to enter the doors of Jannah. For instance, one of the worst immoral acts is pride and boasting. In Surah Luqman, Ayah 18-19, Allah says, "And do not turn your cheek [in contempt] toward people and do not walk through the earth exultantly. Indeed, Allah does not like everyone self-deluded and boastful. And be moderate in your pace and lower your voice; indeed, the most disagreeable of sounds is the voice of donkeys." Imagine yourself being compared to donkeys. Is that truly what you want? Also, in Surah Ar Rahman, Allah says, "And establish weight in justice and do not make deficient the balance." Here, the balance means the balance between good and bad deeds. Tafsir Ibn Kathir said, "He (Allah) created the heavens and earth in justice and truth so that everything is founded on, and observing, justice and truth." this is another reason why it is important to stay upon your good morals. If you are immoral, it tips the balance between good and bad.

To stay away from immoral actions, it is important to understand moral acts that can be done daily. For example, there are many ways I can do moral acts daily. In school, when I get bullied, I just keep my cool and try not to let them get under my skin. I try to stay as quiet and as calm as I can when the teacher is teaching something new and I may be getting impatient. If the teacher is teaching a concept I do not quite understand, I get frustrated. But I keep my frustration in and ask for the teacher's help. When I am in a quarrel with my friends, I try my best not to raise my voice or talk in an angry tone of voice. At home, whenever guests come around, I serve them to their needs and spend time with them. When I am faced with a problem or situation, I don't just look for the easy way out but rather a solution with which I don't do anything immoral. Above all, I stay as optimistic as I can.

Nonetheless, there are many traps that can lead you into doing immoral acts. This includes hanging out with who you think are cool even if they are not so good in their deeds. Never hang out with people who won't help you when you need help because he is not your real friend. As the saying goes," A friend in need is a friend indeed". Despite all these traps, one must remember to be a true Muslim. We must always believe in Allah as the sole creator and sustainer of the universe. Our actions must always reflect upon the fear of Allah and love for him and his creations. One way to prevent yourself from falling into this trap is, find people who are humble, kind, and gentle. Try to befriend those kinds of people because they will be friends worth having. If you ever see your friend in need of assistance and you can help in any way, do so. You won't regret it as Allah is always watching and will know of all the good deeds you have done in your life. In the end, the best of ways to be moral is to follow the example of the Prophet (saw), his companions, and the Quran.

References:
1. https://www.islamicity.org/12534/5-ahadith-about-good-character/
2. https://www.islamreligion.com/articles/1943/morality-and-ethics-in-islam/
3. https://www.whyislam.org/islam/morality-ethics-in-islam/

THIRD PLACE
Shehbaz Khan, Ellicott City, Md.
Bonnie Branch Middle School

In our day-to-day life, we interact with people who are different from us totally, whether it be race, religion, culture, experiences, or any combination in between, and they have their own moral values, which they change in accordance to their interests. Islamic moral values have a divine source, therefore they can never be manipulated. In this essay, I will explain why it is important to maintain moral values and over come undertakings, along with my experiences.

Being Muslims, it is our prime responsibility to carry out Allah's commandments to earn in his pleasure, no matter where we are, and thus, Islamic moral values are a major aspect. I go to a public school, and I see different kinds of people. They may act differently, and I have to have good working relationships with everyone, keeping Islamic values in mind and not letting middle school norms take over. Prophet Muhammad (saw) once said:

"Righteousness is good morality, and wrongdoing is that which wavers in your soul and which you dislike people finding out about." ("Forty Hadith" by An-Nawawi, Hadith 27)

As part of maintaining moral values, we should also avoid using non Islamic values. For example, this could be following a worldly norm in order to not seem different from others. About a year ago, around the time of the winter holidays, my French teacher was showing us how to make christmas trees out of paper. I did not want to do this, even though everyone else was, for fear of not following Allah's orders. I politely told her I didn't want to make one, because Allah (swt) said in the Quran: "O you who believe! Fear Allah as he should be feared and do not die except as believers." (Al-Quran 3:102)

There are many ways we can overcome undertakings. One way is to speak out with your voice, and use your actions that you have learned as a Muslim. One day in math class, my teacher passed back our quizzes, and I was happy to see I had a hundred. As I flipped through the quiz, I realized I had made a mistake that my teacher had not notice. My thoughts fought against each other, one saying I should not draw my teacher's attention to this, and the other saying to be honest. I asked myself, do I really deserve this hundred? When my heart said no, I went up to my teacher, and I told her about it, even though all of my classmates tried to stop me. She took half a point off, but it didn't matter to me, because I chose Allah's pleasure over just half a point, and honesty is a very important moral value. Allah (swt) said in the Qur'an: "And do not mix truth with falsehood or knowingly conceal the truth." (Al-Quran 2:42)

Even if we understand the good parts of following Islamic values, we still have to know the consequences if we do not follow. If I did not keep my limits when talking to my peers at my school, I would be engulfed in middle school norms. If I did make the Christmas trees, I would not seem different, but I would earn Allah's anger. If I had not told my teacher about the mistake on my quiz, I would have hidden the truth.

The moral values of Islam are the guidelines to how we should live our lives as Muslims. If we look profoundly into this set of laws, we discover that these laws will not only make us earn Allah (Swt)'s pleasure, but it will also make this world a better place to live, with peace, harmony, and justice.

HIGH SCHOOL - COLLEGE, LEVEL 5
Grades 9 & 10

Civility, Ethics, and Morality

You see incidents of unethical, immoral, and uncivil behaviors around, manifested through hatred, racism, and intolerance. Instead of being negatively impacted by these, think about how you can use Islamic teachings in promoting common shared values of ethics, morality and civility in public sphere.

FIRST PLACE
Ibrahim Khan, Ellicott City, Md.
River Hill High School

"Build a Wall and Keep the Mexicans out!", "Washington Post journalist, Khashoggi Murdered", "Eleven Jews murdered in Pittsburgh Synagogue!", "Ousted Prime Minister of Pakistan Jailed for Corruption Charges." "Maryland – One of Top Five States with Opioid Overdose Related Deaths". These are the top headlines that we are surrounded by on the news. The moral degradation in our society isn't just affecting non-muslims, but it is also affecting muslims as well. As believers, what can we do to combat evil that lurks within our communities and society at large? We must counter the declining moral values in society with Islamic teachings, by softening our hearts, taking action by enjoining good, and promoting understanding and clearing up misconceptions.

One way we can address immorality is checking the state of our hearts. One of the biggest problems is that we are forgetting our Lord and our true purpose in this world, to worship Allah. We are getting distracted by things that are short-term and will go away. In Surah Hashr verse 19 Allah (swt) says *And be not like those who forgot Allah, so He made them forget themselves. Those are the defiantly disobedient.* If we get distracted by worldly things, then we may forget about Allah and our hearts will harden. In the pursuit of money, instagram followers, fantasy football, we might be "tricked" into doing immoral acts such as lying, deceiving, cheating and even worse, shirk.

In Surah As-Shura, verse 89, Allah (swt) says *But only one who (will prosper) comes to Allah with a sound heart.* We must avoid poisoning our heart with immoral acts and remember Allah (swt) in everything we do. Whether it may be to recite Quran everyday for a few minutes or to make dua. We also need to wake up our hearts by thinking about people who are less fortunate than us. Once I went to Baltimore to a shelter to volunteer and I witnessed how many people did not have homes and were lacking basic necessities. When I saw them, 1 I was very grateful to Allah (Swt) for everything that I had like food, shelter, and clothes. If we live in the mindset that everything we have is a gift from Allah, then we will be more grateful for the things that we have and it will keep our hearts full of life and iman.

The next strategy to combat evil is to encourage the doing of good actions through being a positive role model. Allah says in surah Imran ayah 104: *And let there be [arising] from you a nation inviting to [all that is] good, enjoining what is right and forbidding what is wrong, and those will be the successful.*

One problem in society is that people can't differentiate between right and wrong because they have been doing immoral actions their whole life. We can teach others to kind, thoughtful, truthful, and generous through our actions. For example, most high schoolers use curse words and bad language. Your friends will pick up that you don't curse or you don't talk bad about others, and over time, they will change their ways as well. On the authority of Abu Musa al-Ash'ari (ra), the Prophet (saw) said:

> "The likeness of a righteous friend and an evil friend, is the likeness of a (musk) perfume seller and a blacksmith. As for the perfume seller, he may either bestow something on you, or you may purchase something from him, or you may benefit from his sweet smell. And as for the blacksmith, he may either burn your clothes, or you may be exposed to his awful smell." [Bukhari and Muslim].

We can be like the perfume seller and when we are with our friends, we can rub our good character onto them. Being a positive role model leaves a long-lasting impression on others as doing good is contagious.

The last way that we can fight immoral actions is by educating others and clearing up misconceptions. The problem is that people develop misunderstandings about each other due to media outlets or other sources, resulting in hate and fear. One incident caused by lack of understanding was the Pittsburgh synagogue shooting which killed 11 people. The shooter was motivated by hate and lacked understanding of the Jewish faith because of what he read on social media. Likewise, the only perception of Muslims some people develop is negative and hostile due to the inaccurate and biased media coverage. Repercussions of misinformation can cause people to be harsh on their neighbors even though they have never met them. The solution to this issue is to go outside and be our best selves. If you hear someone in school speaking falsely about your religion, it is essential that you speak up in order to correct their misconceptions.. This, in turn, can cause a ripple effect through your peers allowing them to correctly understand Islam and its practices. We should also teach our fellow Muslims the importance of having good character when interacting with Muslims and non-muslims to help them improve their morals.

Islam is the solution to the moral degradation that surrounds us. We must counter the evil by having empathy with those who are oppressed, by doing good and being a positive role model for others, and last but not least, by spreading the truth and promoting understanding of the deen. We should uphold moral values as Allah has commanded in the Quran and follow the example of the Prophet Muhammad (saw). The result of us practicing the character of the Prophet (saw) and spreading truth will not only benefit us in this life with positive relations and happiness, but also in the hereafter, earning Allah's pleasure and being rewarded with jannah.

References:
1. Hilālī, T. A., Khan, M. M., & Bukhārī, M. I. (2010). Interpretation of the meanings of the noble Quran in the English language:. Darussalam.
Hadith Collection. (n.d.). Retrieved from http://www. hadithcollection.com/

SECOND PLACE
Sawdah Munir, Ellicott City, Md.
Mount Hebron High School

Moral Values in Islam: the Hijab and Secularization

The modern era has seen a decline in structured moral values in the Muslim Ummah, and collective society, due to the progressive absence of concurrent ethics in both liberalism and conservatism in relation to Islam. Because Western liberalism is often dismissive of enforced principles, and conservatism is increasingly associated with prejudice, Muslims are left with a constant struggle to find the appropriate middle ground. Hence, the ethics of secularization and its multitude of meanings come into debate, catching Islam in its crossfire. A prominent example is the discourse surrounding the hijab. Not only is hijab questioned for its supposed encroachment on a secular society, the continually prominent liberal mindset labels restrictions in garment as coherent with the misogynistic values of the politically conservative, which society agrees to disdain. Before the specific influences of the non-Muslim world can be assessed, however, one must first evaluate the growing trend of Muslims arguing their differing ideals rather than cultivating the similarities that unite them as an Ummah, rendering them unable to grow into an exemplar model of morality.

Within the Muslim community, advocates vouch for secularization, believing religious practices should remain separate from the public sphere. These vouches manifest in the form of support for the hijab bans that have appeared worldwide. To preface, this issue should not be confused with the heated debate of the obligation of the hijab itself, which is acceptably open for scholarly contentions. Through a modern lens, critics scrutinize the origins of the veil, disregarding these analyses. One columnist, named Qanta Ahmed (2017), voices an argument shared by many, asserting that the veil is in fact a misogynistic ideal that is falsely based on the Qur'an, which she believes only asks women to cover their chests. Ahmed

(2017) adds that the veil is more oppressive than freeing, and if it is banned, no rights are being infringed upon. Like many others who share her opinion, Ahmed neglects to realize the further complexities of the issue, that the hijab for Muslim women extends beyond the stereotype that is most pleasing to the Western eye. An entry from Oxford Islamic Studies points out that the ideal of modesty in Islam is not restricted to attire but also largely consists of presenting a serious and humble manner when in public (Guindi and Zuhur, n.d.). Especially in modern society, the hijab, it states, is a Muslimah's way of rejecting "Western materialism, commercialism, and values" (Guindi and Zuhur, n.d.). All too often, the Muslim community is lost in the appeal of being swept along in the next movement of social justice, sacrificing Islamic values for the more Western ideal of a blissful existence being found in the absence of moderation. In fact, it is narrated that the Prophet (saw) said that "Haya' (pious shyness from committing religious indiscretions) does not bring anything except good" (The Hadith, n.d.). It is not shameful to preserve the sanctity of one's body and shy away from boisterous actions, rather it is valued by God and allows for a balanced and righteous society.

Facilitating civil discussions in the Muslim community will encourage youth to gain a better understanding of how they may fit into their environment as American Muslims and be provided answers from a learned source instead of the misleading depths of the internet. An opportunity at their local mosque, for example, allowing such discussion can open a doorway for learning both the logic and beauty behind the teachings of Islam, when all too often a child is met with simply the weight of obligation; the youth should know that Islam is a religion of ease and not of strict rules and regulations. Perhaps then, the inclination to shy away from the importance of constraints will fade with time.

Furthermore, the claims against the hijab serve as a justification for the supposed need for Muslims, explicitly women, to contribute to the secular nature of society. Though secular can refer to the separation of religion and state within the government, the term in this context applies more to the acceptability of a discernible presence of religion in the public sphere. Following her argument against hijab, Ahmed (2017) establishes that secularism can allow individuals to practice their religion without input and prejudice. In other words, a woman who can not be outwardly recognized as Muslim is safer in the public sphere, and those surrounding her are not influenced by her beliefs either. Ahmed (2017) summarizes by stating that public areas do not necessitate religion and are harmed by its presence. Yet in direct contrast, Dr. Khalil Abdurrashid (2017), from Yaqeen Institute, illustrates how "in pre-modern societies, Muslim civilizations contained public spaces... where living meant being immersed in social, economic, political, and intellectual conditions that were conducive to a moral and spiritual life". Publicly recognizing the existence of a higher entity historically benefited and guided historic societies towards a better moral understanding (Abdurrashid 2017). Modern secularism has resulted in dire consequences for the way the Muslim mind and soul now perceives the world, and Abdurrashid (2017) reflects that even though "we ask moral questions just as our predecessors did," the questions "are different because of the conditions that give rise to [them] push us to cast doubt on the answer even before that answer is produced". The visibility of the hijab is irrelevant to the harmony of society, and instead can promote the cultivation of religion-based conversation, a truer path to unanimity where people may reach more understanding about each other and their own spiritual beliefs. These types of dialogues outside and within the Muslim community present a manifestation of Abdurrashid's (2017) solution: instilling a deeper certainty in the belief of God. God's presence around humanity is undeniable, so there is no reason to conceal it any setting, public or private.

In the face of moral degradation, the Muslim Ummah faces the challenge of overcoming society's strict polarization of ideals, where each side is isolated to the point where only those who share their opinions are correct. It is easy to become swept up in this political battlefield, adhering completely to one side's ideals. As American Muslims in a modern society, moral guidance is found in first in the teachings of Islam, especially the Qur'an, where the word of God trumps all.

References
1. El Guindi, F., & Zuhur, S. (n.d.). Hijāb. Retrieved January 5, 2019, from Oxford Islamic Studies.
2. http://www.oxfordislamicstudies.com/article/opr/t236/e0306
3. Ahmed, Q. (2017, March 18). As a muslim, I strongly support the right to ban the veil. Retrieved January 4, 2019, from The Spectator website: https://www.spectator.co.uk/2017/03/the-right-to-ban-the-veil-is-good-news-for-everybody-including-muslims/
4. Abdurrashid, K. (2017, February 20). Islam and the secular age: Between certainty and uncertainty. Retrieved January 6, 2019, from Yaqeen Institute website: https://yaqeeninstitute.org/en/khalil-abdurrashid/islam-and-the-secular-age-between-certainty-and-uncertainty/
5. The Hadith, (pp. Sahih Bukhari, Book 78, Hadith Number 144).

THIRD PLACE
Musa Ahmad, Lanham, Md.
Homeschool

In our world today, we are surrounded by people of immorality and incivility. We live in a world that is filled with hatred, racism, greed, corruption, and intolerance. People's lives are being taken because of the color of their skin, economic inequality is at its peak, our politicians are corrupted by love for power and ignore society's needs, and family values are at stake. The fundamental cause of all of these problems is that people have lost their faith. A person without any beliefs or faith is unquestionably lost. Of course, Islam is the true path, but people who follow any religion tend to be more focused, kind, and civil because all religions encourage ethical, moral, and civil behavior. Therefore as Muslims, it is our obligation to show people and spread the beautiful message of Islam. In this essay, I will first look into the Islamic teachings and guidelines to find solutions to these issues and then give practical steps that we can implement in our day to day lives with our own behavior internally and our relationship with others.

Allah (swt) says in the Quran "Indeed, Allah orders justice and good conduct and giving to relatives and forbids immorality and bad conduct and oppression. He admonishes you that perhaps you will be reminded." (Al-Quran 16:90) In this ayah, Allah (swt) forbids us from immorality and bad conduct or incivility. Allah (swt) also commands us to justice which is the foundation of civility. We tend to love this Dunya so much that we become delusional and we start to worship our desires. We are taught in the Quran that "... this worldly life is not but diversion and amusement. And indeed, the home of the Hereafter - that is the [eternal] life, if only they knew." (Al-Quran 29:64). If we internalize the fact that this dunya is temporary, and that the hereafter is our true destination, we would be much more focused on our deeds rather than our wealth and power. During the time of the Prophet (saw), his situation was very similar to ours today. There were corrupt leaders, greed, and even racism. During that time, the Quraish would even bury their newborn daughters alive. They also used to treat their slaves dreadfully. There was such a tremendous amount of hatred between the tribes that led to multiple wars. That is why Allah (swt) sent the Prophet (saw) to all people so that he could show us how to implement these guidelines into our daily lives. As Muslims, it is the responsibility of each and every one of us to share our profound religion with our society. If we really want to put an end to racism, ignorance, and immorality, we need to follow the Islamic teachings and guidelines.

Aristotle said, "It is during our darkest moments that we must focus to see the light." We can complain day and night about how dreadful our situation is, but that will not really change anything. If we want change in our world, then we need to take action by first changing ourselves and our attitudes in the following three ways. First, we must have a positive attitude. Yes, we all have problems in our lives but we must realize that it could always be worse. America is filled with opportunities that no other countries have and we should take advantage of that. We must stay positive and look at what we have rather than looking at what we do not. Second, we need to educate ourselves about the deen, through studying the Quran and the seerah of the Prophet (saw) which will enable us, and consequently Muslims all over the world, to be an embodiment of good morals, ethics, and civility, as seen in the example of the Prophet (saw). One day, Aisha (ra) was asked by Qatadah about the character of the Prophet (saw) and she replied: "Verily the character of the Prophet of Allah was the Quran."

In order for there to be change in unethical behavior, we need to use the Islamic teachings mentioned above to promote commonly shared values in our society through the following two means. First, we must raise awareness and spread the message of Islam through dawah so that people can understand what Islam really stands for. A tremendous problem in today's society is ignorance. Majority of Americans have no idea what is going on in the rest of the world, nor do they care to know. For example, a month ago the media talked about a dog that accidentally got sent to Japan but they did not even mention the thousands of human beings that are being massacred in Burma and East Turkistan. It is also our responsibility to educate people by arranging seminars to raise awareness. Second, we need to encourage civic engagement. Rather than just sitting back and complaining about our government and people, we should get involved in the government and inspire people. We have freedom of speech so let us use that to better our country.

In conclusion, in order to eradicate unethical, immoral, and uncivil behavior, which is causing turmoil in our world, we must follow the Quran and Sunnah and take action. By having a positive attitude, educating ourselves, being a good example, engaging in dawah, and encouraging civic engagement, we can use Islamic teachings to promote the common good in our society. We need to keep in mind that change starts from within, so if we want society to change, we must start off with ourselves as Allah (swt) mentions in the Quran "Indeed, Allah will not change the condition of a people until they change what is in themselves." (Al-Quran 13:11).

References:
1. Al-Quran (16:90), (29:64), (13:11).
2. Famous Quotes at BrainyQuote. (n.d.). Retrieved January 9, 2019, from https://www.brainyquote.com/
3. Sahih Muslim Hadith #746

HIGH SCHOOL - COLLEGE, LEVEL 5
Grades 11 through College

Civility, Ethics, and Morality

You see incidents of unethical, immoral, and uncivil behaviors around, manifested through hatred, racism, and intolerance. Instead of being negatively impacted by these, think about how you can use Islamic teachings in promoting common shared values of ethics, morality and civility in public sphere.

FIRST PLACE
Nimah Nayel, Rockville, Md.
Richard Montgomery School

Regardless of race, religion, sexuality, everyone has a set of values. Even psychopaths, capable of mass murders, follow a set of personal values. Everyone likes to walk around believing their values their own, unique to them, which is true to a point. However, our values are almost completely derivative, from family, friends, community, religion, etc. This doesn't mean we can blame these sources for the actions we choose to take. We can only understand and move past our mistakes. Thus, in examining the issue of declining morality in America, and worldwide, we must understand that placing blame is virtually ineffective, especially because the blame isn't a point source; we can't point to one thing to justify our collective actions.

In the United States, 113 students died in school shootings in 2018 alone. In 2016, we lost 1,092 victims to unnecessary police brutality. As I write this, innocent Syrians are losing their homes, families, and lives, Palestinians are being brutally attacked, Sudanese citizens are forced to take to the streets mimicking the deadly fight of the French Revolution of almost 250 years ago. We've allowed the ease of the spreading of this information desensitize us. Every hashtag removes some of the personable aspect of the news. Each death doesn't hit us the same way it should, anymore. We should bleed as a unit, as an ummah, but we're often finding ourselves forwarding WhatsApp prayers for the children dying in the Middle East, and then gossiping with our friends in the same breath. Technology isn't all bad, of course, but is like a knife that can be used to slice an apple to give to a poor man, or kill someone. It's not about the tools we're given, but the way we choose to use them.

Abu Huraira reported that the Prophet (saw) said, "Whoever believes in Allah and the Last Day, must either speak good or remain silent." (Muslim Book#18 Hadith #1) Surrounded by negative and hopeless rhetoric describing the ways our society is crumbling, and being faced with the constant reminder of the pain we're surrounded with makes it easy for us to fall into a cycle of negativity. But we must break that cycle. The spreading of good news, of letting our voices only speak positively, elicits change. The counter to my point argues that if we don't discuss the brutality that occurs, we won't be able to make effective decisions. In an age of staying "woke," knowing the details of every attack is becoming an obsession. However, thus far, we've tried that approach. The radio, the television, online articles, social media, dumps negativity on negativity on us at a constant rate, and yet not much has changed. The idea in speaking positively doesn't suggest to live in ignorance - that is to live to blindly. It instead suggests that in discussing real issues, we must synonymously discuss real solutions, delivering hope with each message of despair. We can't ignore the pain our brothers and sisters are going through, but if we make an effort to speak positively, our tongues will speak of the oppression in a way that asks and appeals to change, not just to simply and superficially report on the 'what,' but to discuss the why, and then the how. This is the only way we can ensure that we continue to grow, and never get stuck in that cycle of negativity and inaction. The dialogue will change from a hopeless rhetoric, to real and valuable discussions of solutions.

Rather than shying away from using social media, from mobilizing on the Internet, we need to understand these tools, and be able to use them to further our agenda. In order to do so, however, we need to be confident in our agenda, and this societal degradation of morals has negatively affected our Ummah, especially in the division between the older generation and the youth. It's human nature to attempt to leave or ignore what you don't know- but this attitude burns bridges between parent and child. When parents try to solve their children's difficulties in the same way they solved theirs, a distrust arises, and that distrust often is projected on the child's relationship with Islam. If their parents are preaching from an Islamic standpoint, and they can't relate, then what will motivate them to continue following the teachings of Islam? This disconnect can break our Ummah apart- if we let it. But a tool powerful enough to break apart our Ummah can also work to heal it, strengthen it, and make us the leaders of our future. As aforementioned, we have all the tools to lead the world to our design, as long as we use them correctly. This means focusing more on larger concepts, rather than nitpicking on one another. Backbiting, and judging others, especially others in our community will tear us apart. In a hadith reported by Ali ibn Hussein, the Prophet (saw) said, "Verily, part of perfection in Islam is for a person to leave what does not concern him." (Sunan al-Tirmidhi, 2318) There is a difference between providing advice, and being judgmental, and we cannot walk that line blindly. We need to be well-versed in our religion, in our set of moral codes. We can and will change the world, if we become that change, we want to see ourselves.

One cannot mandate how those around us act, and Allah (swt) doesn't expect us to. It's why on the Day of Judgement, we're held accountable for only one person's actions- our own. If we as an Ummah take on the challenge of maintaining positivity and optimism in the face of adversity and injustice, however, not only are we doing right by our goals in the afterlife, but we will be able to be the leaders and role models, enacting positive change, and strengthening our Ummah. It's difficult to be spat at and smile, but for the sake of our community, for the sake of our morality, for the sake of generations to come, we simply must.

References:
1. Smietana, B. (9 May 2017) Retrieved from https://lifewayresearch.com/2017/05/09/americans-worry-about-moral-decline-cant-agree-on-right-and-wrong/
2. Miller, A. (July 2017) Retrieved from https://www.thetrumpet.com/15831-why-moral-decline-matters
3. Coughlan, S. (12 December 2018) Retrieved from https://www.bbc.com/news/business-46507514
4. Elias, A-A. (4 June 2016) Retrieved from https://abuaminaelias.com/the-marvel-of-positive-thinking-in-islam/

5. Network, G-G. (9 February 2015) Retrieved from https://www.goodnewsnetwork.org/6-quran-quotes-teach-love-tolerance-freedom-religion/

6. Khazan, O. (8 May 2018) Retrieved from https://www.theatlantic.com/health/archive/2018/05/the-57375-years-of-life-lost-to-police-violence/559835/

7. Shah, Z-H. (29 October 2013) Retrieved from https://themuslimtimes.info/2013/10/29/three-hundred-verses-about-compassionate-living-in-the-quran/

SECOND PLACE
Areebah Jahin, Herndon, Va.
Homeschool

Undivided

Dylann Roof went into a historic church in South Carolina and fatally shot nine African Americans. A man in Miami Beach threatened to burn down a condominium and "kill all Jews" inside. A woman was harassed in a public park in Chicago for wearing a shirt with the Puerto Rico flag on it. A Wichita restaurant owned by an immigrant Muslim was burned down, with the words "Go Back" left in graffiti. If you were to read a whole list of hate crimes over the past couple of years in the U.S., it would take days. More than 7,000 hate crimes have been reported in the past year alone. We live in a country where minority groups are prevalent and if we continue to look at our differences, hatred and intolerance will only increase. However, if we could try and focus on our similarities, it is possible to together and unite. We can use Islamic teachings on morality and civility in the public sphere by becoming more open-minded towards those of other faiths, clearing misconceptions of Islam to Non-Muslims, and responding to immoral behavior in the way Islam teaches us.

We can use Islamic teachings on ethics in our society by being more open-minded. Islam is a way of life. It teaches us everything, from what to say when waking up in the morning to how to pray our five daily prayers. It also includes how to act with people from other groups, like our fellow non-Muslims. In Surah Al-An'am, Allah (swt) says, "And do not insult those whom they call upon besides Allah" (Al-Qur'an 6:108). Although we may disagree about many things with non-Muslims, such as their belief in some other God other than Allah (swt), we have no right to disrespect them. We can prevent this by changing the stubborn mindsets that some of us tend to have. If we put an effort to be a little more open-minded, there would be less division between the Muslims and Non-Muslims. Both groups will feel more comfortable with each other, which will slowly ease tensions within our society. Unfortunately, tensions also exist within our own ummah. Our fellow brothers and sisters can be heard saying to their own sister in Islam, "Oh, I can see your hair! Why do you wear the hijab at all if you are not going to wear it the right way?" This "cancelled culture" is so common these days, though we never heard of the Prophet (saw) doing anything like it. We should follow his example and politely correct them when we see something wrong. We all live on this Earth, it is not any of our own, so we have to be respectful towards one another. Only then can we expect it in return.

We can use Islamic teachings on civility in the public sphere through clarifying the misconceptions about Islam held by non-Muslims. A popular stereotype about Muslims is that we support violence. We all know Islam as a religion of peace. However, violence is permitted, but only for certain circumstances where it is necessary, such as protecting our freedom of religion. It is mentioned in Surah Al-Mumtahanah that, "Allah only forbids you from those who fight you because of religion and expel you from your homes and aid in your expulsion – [He forbids] that you make allies of them. And whoever makes allies of them, then it is those who are the wrongdoers" (Al-Qur'an 60:9). Islam does not say to fight non-Muslims, but rather to fight to protect our religious freedom. If they don't do anything to harm us, we have no right to harm them either; Islam prohibits it. The problem is people cherry pick, and they do not look at the whole picture. The other problem is that we ourselves do not know this about our religion. Once we learn it ourselves, then we can let them know. If we told them what the Quran really says, with the whole context, they will be more tolerant and have a better understanding of what Islam really is.

We can use the teachings in Islam about morality in our community by responding to immoral behavior, which we see so much of nowadays, the way Islam taught us. As Allah (swt) says in Surah Al-Ma'idah, "O you who have believed, be persistently standing firm for Allah, witnesses in justice, and do not let the hatred of a people prevent you from being just. Be just; that is nearer to righteousness. And fear Allah; indeed, Allah is Acquainted with what you do" (Al-Qur'an 5:8). Allah (swt) is telling us that although there is hostility all around us, we should not let that come in the way of being equitable as our own person, and as an ummah. As Muslims, we have an image to maintain, especially with the media's negative portrayal of Islam in the current news. Just like we do personally, we have a reputation that we are responsible for. When we see uncivil behavior, we should try our best to respond to it the way Islam taught us, so that the non-Muslims may learn from us.

Morality is a huge aspect of Islam and we can learn a lot about it through the Quran, which has everything we could ever need to know. If we just opened it, read it more often, and understood its meaning, we could become better people. We can use its teachings on morality by being more open-minded, clearing misconceptions, and countering immoral behavior the way Islam teaches us. As Prophet Muhammad (saw) said "...The most generous people after me will be those who will acquire knowledge and then disseminate it" (Al-Tirmidhi, Hadith 93). If we better ourselves through knowledge from the Quran, then we will have the ability to share the light with others.

References:
1. Ali, A. (2011, May). Islam and public morality. Retrieved January 5, 2019, from New Age Islam website: http://www. newageislam.com/islamic-ideology/ islam-and-public-morality/d/4579
2. Does Islam teach hatred and violence. (2017, July 10). Retrieved January 5, 2019, from Why Islam website: https://www. whyislam.org/faqs/does-islam-teach-hatred-and-violence/
3. Eligon, J. (2018, November 13). Hate crimes increase for the third consecutive year, F.B.I. reports. Retrieved January 5, 2019, from The New York Times website:https://www.google.com/ url?q=https://www.nytimes.com/2018/11/13/us/hate-crimes-fbi-2017.html&sa=D&ust=1546657185821000&usg=AFQjCNGa GecyBKhucNKtd7E_J jT12UALvw

THIRD PLACE
Nazifa Mahmud, College Park, Md.
Al Huda School

You see incidents of unethical, immoral, and uncivil behaviors around, manifested through hatred, racism, and intolerance. Instead of being negatively impacted by these, think about how you can use Islamic teachings in promoting common shared values of ethics, morality, and civility in the public sphere.

Immorality is a disease and over time it has turned into an epidemic. It (immorality) is spreading very fast that everyone is getting affected by it. Some of us try to get rid of it, others face it head on, but the majority is so used to being sick that they forget it even exists. However, Allah (swt) has warned us against any acts of hatred in the Quran several times. He says, "O you who have believed, be persistently standing firm for Allah, witnesses in justice, and do not let the hatred of a people prevent you from being just. Be just; that is nearer to righteousness. And fear Allah; indeed, Allah is Acquainted with what you do (Al-Quran 5:8). Thus, it is clear that Muslims should work towards finding a treatment for this disease.

Our societies these days are filled with violence and trauma. From little kids getting bullied in school to teenagers shooting in their own schools to adults committing murder solely for one's beliefs. It has been amongst us for a very long time and it needs to be treated. Uncivil acts need our full attention and the best way to face it is with the clear verses of the Quran and the teachings of the prophet Muhammed (saw).

APPENDIX A

From the EPC Community

Participants in the Essay Panel Contest have shared their experiences, and, in several instances, made efforts to give back to the endeavor by volunteering their own time and areas of expertise. Here are some of their comments.

"I still remember the feeling of butterflies in my stomach before it was my turn to present my speech. There were years where I really didn't want to participate, because for me, writing was always a struggle. But when it came time to speak, there was always this rush of excitement. To this day, I still get butterflies in my stomach before a big presentation, but all the practice that I got from EPC and this platform in general has definitely helped me build my confidence in public speaking, alhamdulillah. I have been apart of EPC for over 12-13 years as a competitor, and now a judge. I love hearing the new voices of our next generation, and seeing the great skills the Muslim youth have to offer MashaAllah."
– Danya Chowdhury, EPC Judge and Past Participant

"It is important that the leaders of tomorrow be able to communicate effectively and with speak confidence, especially in front of large audiences. Starting at a young age, gives our children time for growth and positive feedback. The EPC is a fun and encouraging way to develop these skills and will undoubtedly help them in the future. Thank you for all that you do!"
– Hayder and Humaira Qaadri, EPC Parent

APPENDIX B

EPC Guidelines for 2019

To facilitate uniformity and streamline scoring of the essays, a set of guidelines and standards is provided to each participant prior to the competition. The following details were published for the 2019 Essay Panel Contest.

Essay Writing Guidelines

Definition of an essay – Within the context of this competition, an essay is a four-part paper where the writer takes a stance on the essay question and develops it into a coherent, well organized, and well-thought out composition. The four parts of the essay are:

INTRODUCTION – This part of the paper lays out the "roadmap" for your essay. It explains the question from your understanding and how you plan to handle it. It helps the reader know what to expect and look for in your essay. Usually, the introduction contains the thesis statement. This single sentence is the crux of your essay. It explains your stance on the question and exactly what you will cover in the body of the essay. An introductory paragraph can start out with general information and end with a specific thesis statement.

BODY – This is the "meat" of your essay. In this part, you will thoroughly explain your position. You should use examples, quotes, and any information you have gathered from your research to support your argument. This is where you show your reader you know and understand the topic. Typically, this part will consist of one to three paragraphs, but can have as many paragraphs as the writer wishes.

CONCLUSION – This is the part of the essay where you sum up your position and re-iterate the main points of the essay. There should not really be any new information here that was not covered in the introduction or the body of the paper. In fact, the conclusion could be considered a "mirror-image" of the introduction (i.e., start out specific and end with general idea).

WORKS CITED PAGE – This is a list of sources that you have referred to in your essay or have used as research or background information. It is placed at the end of the paper on a separate page. Although most of the writing will be your own, a lot of it will be based on information you found in books, lectures, websites, etc. Any information you have used in your essay must be clearly cited within the essay and mentioned on your references page. All citations should follow the rules found in a handbook like the APA Format (http://owl.english.purdue.edu/owl/resource/560/01/), although you can use any handbook with which you are familiar. It is very important to cite all sources that you used; otherwise you could be in danger of plagiarism.

Standard Quranic and Ahadith citation format – for Quran citation use (Sura #: Ayah #), and for Hadith, use (Source, Hadith #) or APA format for other sources.

Other important information:
- Make sure your essay responds directly to the assigned topic
- Your essay should be well organized (both in content and structure) and well thought out.
- There should be a clear flow of ideas throughout the essay (i.e., from one sentence to the next and one paragraph to the next.)
- Your ideas should be supported with research that should be referenced correctly.
- Try to be creative and novel in your approach to the topic.
- Essays should be typed and double-spaced.
- Your name or your school's name should not be anywhere in or on the essay.
- Last but never least, pay attention to spelling, grammar, and punctuation.

- Written statements from the parent/guardian and the author confirming that the work was primarily done by the author (Book publication requires that the work is original and their own.

See http://epc.mafiq.org/ for details on EPC Guidelines.

Each participant is required to submit the following Honor Statement along with his/her essay.

EPC HONOR STATEMENT

Name: _____

Grade: _____

Topic: _____

This essay was researched, organized, and written by me with no help or limited help from my parents or others.

_____   _____
Name of Participant   Date

_____   _____
Name of Parent/Guardian   Date

APPENDIX C

Combined Participant List
for EPC 2017, EPC 2018, EPC 2019

Participants in the 2017-2019 Essay Panel Contests run the gambit of ages and backgrounds from public and private schools across the region in Maryland, Virginia, District of Columbia, Delaware and North Carolina. We congratulate all of them for their efforts to further both their communication skills and the understanding of their deen. They are listed below.

Name	School Name	Residence

Elementary School, Level 1, Grades 1 & 2

Name	School Name	Residence
Sami Abu-Ragheb	Candlewood Elementary	Derwood, MD
Merium Ahmad	DCA (Homeschool)	Lanham, MD
Sumayyah Ahmad	Al Minar Academy	Herndon, VA
Yusha Ahmed	ADAMS	Sterling, VA
Mustafaa Ahmed	M&M Learning Center	College Park, MD
Muhsin Ahmed	Al-Fatih Academy	Reston, VA
Hakeem Ahmed	ADAMS Radiant Hearts Academy	Sterling, VA
Taha Akhtar	Ronald McNair Elementary	Germantown, MD
Uthman Ali	Glenridge Elementary School	Lanham, MD
Anas Ali	Homeschool	Gaithersburg, MD
Hamza-Syed Ali	Homeschool	Gaithersburg, MD
Abdul Rahman Esayed	Al Huda School	College Park, MD
Mariam Ezzeldin	Al-Huda School	College Park, MD
Eman Hamed	Cardinal Ridge Elementary	Centreville, VA
Noor-Al-Haya Hussain	King Abdullah Academy	Herndon, VA
Sarah Imam	Al-Rahmah School	Catonsville, MD
Mehreen Jameel	Al-Rahmah School	Baltimore, MD
Zahara Khan	M&M Learning Center	College Park MD
Harun Khan	Tarbiyah Academy	Elkridge, MD
Hafsah Khan	Al Huda School	College Park, MD
Ismail Khan	Tarbiyah Academy	Lanham, MD
Sanari Khermiche	M&M Learning Center	College Park, MD

Name	School Name	Residence
Zahara Khermiche	M&M Learning Center	College Park, MD
Saad Mahfuz	Homeschool	Greenbelt, MD
Ayesha Mahmood	Mt. Eagle Elementary School	Alexandria, VA
Yusuf Mehmood	MCC, Bushy Park Elementary	Glenelg, MD
Mariyah Mehmood	MCC, Bushy Park Elementary	Glenelg, MD
Alisha Mia	Maryum Islamic Center	Columbia, MD
Safa Munir	Tarbiyah Academy	Elkridge, MD
Hamza Nassef	Homeschool	Winston Salem, NC
Ahmed Nayel	Al Huda School	College Park, MD
Fahim Pagen	Tarbiyah Academy	Elkridge, MD
Zaheen Pathan	ICCL Academy	Laurel, MD
Zakariya Qaadri	QSA (Homeschool)	Lanham, MD
Alisha Reza	Islamic Center of Maryland	Gaithersburg, MD
Arwaa Weathersby	Al Huda School	Bowie, MD
Arwaa Weathersby	M&M Learning Center	College Park, MD

Elementary School, Levels 2, Grades 3 & 4

Name	School Name	Residence
Fatimah Ahmad	Al Minar Homeschool Academy	Herndon, VA
Mustafaa Ahmed	M&M Learning Center	College Park, MD
Saadiq Ahmed	M&M Learning Center	College Park, MD
Ismael Ahmed	Lowes Island Elementary	Sterling, VA
Cali Ali	Glenridge Elementary School	Lanham, MD
Samera Ali	Glenridge Elementary School	Lanham, MD
AbdurRahman Ali	Homeschool	Gaithersburg, MD
Tasneem-Syeda Ali	Homeschool	Gaithersburg, MD
Lina Amiri	ICCL Academy	Laurel, MD
Halima Bandarkar	Al Fatih Academy	Reston,VA
Yusrah Baqqi-Barrett	Baqqi Academy	Laurel, MD
Mahrus Chowdhury	Islamic Center of Maryland	Gaithersburg, MD
Omar Esayed	Al Huda School	College Park, MD
Ali Ezzeldin	Al-Huda School	College Park, MD
Zakariya Faisal	Al-Huda School	College Park, MD
Aia Hamed	Cardinal Ridge Elementary	Centreville, VA
Noor Husain	Al Huda School	College Park, MD
Hanaya Hussain	King Abdullah Academy	Herndon, VA
Ahmad Imam	Homeschool	Catonsville, MD
Muhammad	ISA and ibn Taymiya	Glenarden , MD
Ruwad Islam	Al Huda School	College Park, MD
Talha Jafri	Travilah Elementary School	Potomac, MD

Name	School Name	Residence
Maheen Kamal	Al-Rahmah School	Baltimore, MD
Hafsah Khan	Tarbiyah Academy	Elkridge, MD
Shabbir Khan	Al-Rahmah School	Windsor Mill, MD
Shaheer Khan	Tarbiyah Islamic School	Newark, DE
Noor Mahmood	Mountain View Elementary	Haymarket, VA
Asma Farheen Manzoor	Al-Minar Academy	Herndon, VA
Mohammed Marzouqullah	Al Fatih Academy	Reston, VA
Yusuf Mehmood	MCC Weekend School	Silver Spring, MD
Mariyah Mehmood	MCC Weekend School	Silver Spring, MD
Huda Nassar	Clarksville Elementary	Clarksville, MD
Haneen Nassef	Homeschool	Winston Salem, NC
Namir Pagen	Tarbiyah Academy	Elkridge, MD
Tayzon Hasanati	Pannell Hurt Langdon Campus	Washington DC
Zakariya Qaadri	QSA Homeschool	Lanham, MD
Dawud Qaadri	QSA Homeshool	Lanham, MD
Yusef Seidahmed	Al-Huda School	College Park, MD
Muwahid Trowell	M&M Learning Center	College Park, MD
Khalid Weathersby	M&M Learning Center	College Park, MD

Middle School, Levels 3, Grades 5 & 6

Name	School Name	Residence
Arwa Abedullaziz	Al Huda School	Springfeild, VA
Rayyan Abrahim	Al Huda School	College Park, MD
Deemah Abusway	Al Rahmah School	Baltimore, MD
AbdurRahman Ahmad	Al Minar Academy	Herndon, VA
Hadia Ahmad	Springhill Lake Elementary	Greenbelt, MD
Aarez Ahmad	Al Rahmah School	Baltimore, MD
Saadiq Ahmed	M&M Learning Center	College Park, MD
Raihan Ahmed	Al Rahmah School	Baltimore, MD
Maisha Alam	Al-Minar	Sterling, VA
Rana Alhandali	Al-Qalam Acadamy	Fairfax, VA
Emira-Syeda Ali	Homeschool	Gaithersburg, MD
Marwa Aligabi	Al-Huda School	College Park, MD
Jenna Awadallah	Al Rahmah School	Baltimore, MD
Sarah Azad	Forestville Elementary School	Great Falls,VA
Yusrah Baqqi-Barrett	Baqqi Academy	Laurel, MD
Safiyyah Baqqi-Barrett	Baqqi Academy	Laurel, MD
Sheikha Bazara	Al Qalam Academy	Springfield, VA
Erum Chaudhri	Al Rahmah School	Baltimore, MD
Mahrus Chowdhury	Islamic Center of Maryland	Gaithersburg, MD

Name	School Name	Residence
Nabeel Chowdhury	Al Huda School	College Park, MD
Zaneb Ebrahim	Al Rahmah School	Baltimore, MD
ibraheem Esayed	Al Huda School	College Park, MD
Areeb Gani	Takoma Park Middle School	Silver Spring, MD
Hafsa Hasan	Al-Rahmah School	Baltimore, MD
Sajid Huda	Al Huda School	College Park, MD
Syeda Hussain	Al Rahmah School	Baltimore, MD
Ahmad Imam	Homeschool	Catonsville, MD
Mahir Ishtiaq	Al Rahmah School	Baltimore, MD
Ruwad Islam	Al Huda School	College Park, MD
Nashmia Jaharan	Al-Minar Academy	Herndon, VA
Maheen Kamal	Al Rahmah School	Baltimore, MD
Afsah Kamran	Al-Huda School	College Park
Hartim Katende	Al-Rahmah School	Baltimore, MD
Ayyub Khan	Clarksville Middle School	Clarksville, MD
Mujtaba Khan	ADAMS	Sterling, VA
Shabbir Khan	Al-Rahmah School	Baltimore, MD
Asiya Khan	Tarbiyah Academy	Elkridge, MD
Shehbaz Khan	Bonnie Branch Middle School	Ellicott City, MD
Duriya Khan	Al-Rahmah school	Catonsville, MD
Sulayman Khan	Tarbiyah Academy	Elkridge, MD
Shahana Khan	Tarbiyah Islamic School	Newark, DE
Amina Khan	Al-Rahmah School	Baltimore, MD
Shehbaz Khan	Al-Rahmah School	Catonsville, MD
Cajabo-Sophia Koczela	Al-Rahmah School	Baltimore, MD
Maryam Lee	Al-Rahmah School	Baltimore, MD
Hasan Maharoof	Al-Rahmah School	Baltimore, MD
Saifullah Mahmood	Springfield Estate Elementary	Springfield, VA
Nishaat Makandar	Al-Rahmah School	Baltimore, MD
Marum Malik	Al Rahmah School	Baltimore, MD
Sheila Matumla	Al-Rahmah School	Baltimore, MD
Nimat Mehedi	Al-Qalam Academy	Springfield, VA
Lama Mohamed	Al-Huda School	Silver Spring, MD
Habeebah Nassef	Homeschool	Winston Salem, NC
Dawud Qaadri	QSA (Homeschool)	Lanham, MD
Aima Raza	Al-Rahmah School	Baltimore, MD
Noor Raza	Al-Huda School	College Park, MD
Faseeh Rehman	Al Rahmah School	Baltimore, MD
Khadijah Samiya	Greenbelt Middle School	Greenbelt, MD
Nubaid Shaik	AL-Minar Academy	Sterling, VA

Name	School Name	Residence
Ali Sherif	Al-Rahmah School	Baltimore, MD
Taha Siddiqi	ADAMS Center	Sterling, VA
Afrah Siddiqui	Homeschool	Greenbelt, MD
Lina Tagouri	Al Huda School	College Park, MD
Khalid Weathersby	Al Huda School	Bowie, MD
Rafia Zafar	Al-Rahmah School	Baltimore, MD

Middle School, Levels 4, Grades 7 & 8

Mohammed Abdul-Mujeeb	Homeschool	Laurel, MD
Fadia Abker	Al-Huda School	College Park, MD
Khadijah Ahmad	Al-Minar Homeschool Academy	Herndon, VA
Jinan Ahmad	Al-Minar Homeschool Academy	Herndon, VA
Musa Ahmad	Homeschool	Lanham, MD
Noorah Ahmed	Beltsville Academy	College Park, MD
Dahlia Ahmed	Al Huda School	College Park, MD
Rakin Ahmed	Hafiz Samiullah Quran Institute	Sterling, VA
Emira-Syeda Ali	Homeschool	Gaithersburg, MD
Ramlah Amsa	Al-Huda School	College Park, MD
Asma Amsa	Al- Huda School	College Park, MD
Israah Ansari	Al-Huda School	College Park, MD
Layla Ashkar	Al-Huda School	College Park, MD
Hamza Ashraf	Trailside Middle Schools	Ashburn, VA
Omar Ashraf	TrailSide Middle School	Ashburn, VA
Amina Bandarkar	Al Fatih Academy	Reston,VA
Safiyyah Baqqi-Barrett	Baqqi Academy	Laurel, MD
Zakia Bharde	Al-Huda School	College Park, MD
Nailah Buck	Al-Huda School	College Park, MD
Nabeel Chowdhury	Al Huda School	Greenbelt, MD
Hanan Debencho	Al Huda School	Takoma Park
Khadija Diallo	Al-Huda School	College Park, MD
Asiyah Diao	Al Huda School	Maryland MD
Maryam Elfadly	Al-Huda School	College Park, MD
Yara Hamed	Mercer Middle School	Aldie, VA
Erfan Hamza	Al Huda School	College Park, MD
Samirah Huda	AlHuda School	College Park, MD
Farina Hussain	Al Huda School	College Park, MD
Shaheer Imam	Al-Rahmah School	Baltimore, MD
Muhammad Islam	Al-Huda School	College Park, MD
Maryam Iyer	Al Huda School	College Park, MD

Name	School Name	Residence
Saad Jameel	Al Rahmah School	Baltimore, MD
Afaan Kamran	Homeschool	Bowie, MD
Huda Kemal	Al-Huda School	College Park, MD
Sumeya Kemal	Al-Huda School	College Park, MD
Shehbaz Khan	Bonnie Branch Middle School	Ellicott City, MD
Sulayman Khan	CMIT Academy North	Laurel, MD
Yusuf Khan	DCA Hifz School	Lanham, MD
ibrahim Khan	Clarksville Middle	Clarksville, MD
Ammar Khawaja	Al Huda School	College Park, MD
Simalee Lenssa	Al-Huda School	College Park, MD
Aseal Maatoug	Al-Huda School	College Park, MD
Zayd Mahfuz	DCA (Turkish Hifzh School)	Greenbelt, MD
Lama Mohamed	Al Huda School	Silver Spring, MD
Hala Mohammedaman	Al-Huda School	College Park, MD
Maryum Moin	Excellance Academy	Springfield, VA
Adam Moumena	Al-Huda School	College Park, MD
Diyanah Musabbir	Al-Huda School	Silver Spring, MD
Isabella Naimi	Al-Huda School	College Park,MD
Jannah Nassar	Clarksville Middle School	Clarksville, MD
Widad Nayel	Eastern Middle School	Silver Spring, MD
Aisha Oyedokun	Al Huda School	College Park, MD
Afreen Reza	Islamic Center of Maryland	Gaithersburg, MD
Yasmin Said	Al-Huda School	College Park, MD
Tajammul Saleem	Al Huda School	College Park, MD
Haniya Salih	Al Huda School	College Park, MD
Numan Salih	Al Huda School	College Park, MD
Ameerah Suhail	Al Huda School	College Park, MD
Rayanah Williams	M&M Learning Center	College Park, MD
Rida Zurga	Al Huda School	College Park, MD

High School, Levels 5, Grades 9 & 10

Musa Ahmad	Homeschool	Lanham, MD
Adam Ahmad	Homeschool	Lanham, MD
Nasrin Ali	Al Huda School	College Park, MD
Israah Ansari	Al Huda School	College Park, MD
Suad Esayed	Al Huda School	College Park, MD
Ayman Fatima	Al-Huda School	Laurel, MD
Erfan Hamza	Al Huda School	College Park, MD
Amal Hossain	College Park Academy	Hyattsville, MD

Name	School Name	Residence
Samirah Huda	Thomas Wootton High School	Rockville, MD
Sajid Huda	Thomas Wootton High School	Silver Spring, MD
Sajid Huda	Al Huda School	Silver Spring, MD
Shaheer Imam	Western School of Technology & Environmental Science	Catonsville, MD
Danyah Imam	Western School of Technology & Environmental Science	Catonsville, MD
Radiah Islam	Reservoir High School	Fulton, MD
Areebah Jahin	Lake Braddock Secondary	Burke, VA
Mustafa Khalid	Eleanor Roosevelt High School	Greenbelt, MD
ibrahim Khan	River Hill High School	Clarksville, MD
Zayd Khan	River Hill High School	Clarksville, MD
Aseal Maatoug	Al-Huda School	College Park MD
Zayd Mahfuz	DCA (Turkish Hifzh School)	Lanham, MD
Nazifa Mahmud	Al Huda School	Greenbelt, MD
Ayesha Mirza	Excellence Academy	Alexandria, VA
MajdoleenMohammedaman	Homeschool	Silver Spring, MD
Sawdah Munir	Mount Hebron High School	Ellicott City, MD
Maryum Nassar	River Hill High School	Clakrsville, MD
Ramisa Resha	Lee High School	Springfield, VA

High School, Levels 6, Grades 11 through College

Name	School Name	Residence
Adam Ahmad	Homeschool	Lanham, MD
Afaaf Ahmad	Homeschool	Lanham, MD
Huma Chowdhury	Al Huda School	College Park, MD
Areebah Jahin	Lake Braddock Secondary	Burke, VA
Irfaan Jamarussadiq	Eleanor Roosevelt High School	Greenbelt, MD
Zayd Khan	River Hill High School	Clarksville, MD
Nazifa Mahmud	Al Huda School	College Park, MD
Daiyan Musabbir	Al-Huda School	College Park, MD
Nimah Nayel	Richard Montgomery High	Rockville, MD
Ramisa Resha	Lee High School	Springfield, VA

APPENDIX D

Our Respected Judges – Past and Present

Abdul Mukheeth (Past Category Lead) is a scientist and has judged EPC in the past.

Abu Syed Mahfuz is an author and published 5 books, including forthcoming book on Software Quality, Information Security and Audit, to be published by International Publisher Taylor & Francis Group. Information Technology Professional, Hewlett Packard Enterprise. He has Masters in Software Management, University of Detroit Mercy, Michigan and another Masters in Shariah Law from International Islamic University Malaysia. He is the editor and Publisher of Bangla Amar Newspaper for 10 years.

Ameenah Cowels is currently an English teacher at Al-Huda School, College Park, MD. She has been teaching at Al-Huda for the past three years. She is married; she has four daughters and one cat. Ameenah received her BA from Rowan University in English and Secondary Education. Prior to getting her degree, Ameenah spent 20 years in the United States Air Force as a Public Health Technician and she provided public health, communicable disease and food handling education. During her tour in England, Ameenah and her family reverted to Islam.

Amirah Ahmad (EPC 2019 Category Lead) is an undergraduate student. Amreen Ahmed has recently relocated to Maryland. For me, this is an opportunity to get involved in my new community, and I hope to be able to contribute in the future, in shaa Allah. As a young Muslim, I see events like these as an opportunity to engage our youth, help their spiritual growth and keep them involved in the community.

Anum Shami (EPC 2018 Category Lead) resides in Msrylsnf. She is a mom of three (9 year old, 8 year old and 5 year old). Anum is a clinical pharmacist at University of Maryland, Medical Center. She is also the founder of Muslim Scouts of Maryland. The group aims to give back to the community through service activities and creates a safe and creative place for the young kids.

Arif Kabir (EPC 2018 Category Lead) works as a Senior Consultant for IBM, holds a B.S. in Operations Management & Information Systems, and has completed his memorization of the Qur'an alhamdulillah. He is the Editor-in-Chief of Muslim Youth Musings, an online literary magazine for youth. He has a passion for spreading literature and therefore would love to spread the work of EPC.

Asim Ghafoor has over two decades of experience in advising public policymakers and clients on a variety of legal, political, and trade issues. He is a frequent speaker at seminars, conferences, and in the media on topics of law enforcement, international affairs, finance and politics. He has spoken at Harvard, the University of Virginia School of Law, and Chicago's Kent College of Law. Previously, Mr. Ghafoor worked in the Texas House of Representatives, giving him great insight into the legislative and law-making process. From 1997-2000, Asim Ghafoor served as Legislative Assistant to Congressman Ciro D. Rodriguez (D-TX) and advised the Congressman on a variety of issues, including international affairs, banking, civil rights, transportation, armed services and veterans' affairs. Mr. Ghafoor earned his JD from the University of Texas School of Law. He is married and has three children.

Doha Nassar is a sophomore at the University of Maryland College Park studying Elementary Education. She started competing in EPC when she was in third grade and has seen how much the competition helped improve my writing and speech skills. Therefore, she decided that it was time to give back to the organization that has done so much for me by helping them judge this year.

Gibran Ali is a software engineer by profession. "I graduated from the University of Maryland College Park in December 2012, majoring in Computer Science. I am also the program coordinator at the Youth Group at the Prince George's Muslim Association. I believe that the EPC is a very powerful platform through which the youth can express themselves and learn the skills required to become leaders in the community. I will be judging the media competition at the EPC and will try my best to be as fair and reasonable as possible."

Hasannah Ali (EPC 2018 Category Lead) is currently teaching 1st grade at Al-Huda School. "I have my degree in Psychology and I'm pursuing a higher degree in Educational Psychology at UMBC. Having attended Al-Huda and a local homeschooling program, I participated in EPC several times and have even been a part of their panel discussion."

Hasan Ahmed is a scientist and attorney by training. "The ability to construct a compelling narrative is critical to communicating ideas. EPC is designed to challenge our youth to harness their language skills, critical thinking, and creativity and produce a work which inspires. The next generation of Muslims must inspire the world with their ideas so that the truth about Islam is known to all. I am honored to participate in this noble effort to prepare our youth for the monumental challenges they will face as they engage the world."

Hena Zuberi is the Editor-in-Chief of Muslimmatters.org, an award winning web magazine. A community organizer for years, she resides in the Washington DC metro, with her husband and four children, where she is the staff reporter for the Muslim Link newspaper. Hena transitioned from television into print and social journalism after working as a TV news reporter and producer for

CNBC Asia and World Television News (now Associated Press TV). Most recently, Hena's work has been published in the Tree of Life – a resource book by CHAI Parenting Initiative, a nonprofit dedicated to mental health and wellness in the South Asian community. She was featured on American Public Media's radio show, The Story, and has spoken at the Society of Professional Journalists Conference. Hena served as the Youth Director at the Unity Center in Southern California for ten years. She uses her experience with youth to conduct Growing Up with God workshops in communities around the country.

Imam Ali Siddiqui teaches Islam, comparative religion, History of Islam and Muslims of Americas, contemporary issues to Muslims and non-Muslims at the institutions of higher learning as a Visiting Faculty including Sonoma State, Santa Rosa Community College, School of Religion (Claremont Graduate University), California Baptist University, Disciple of Christ Seminary, School of Theology (now Lincoln University), and La Verne University, and Open University Denver. He has been on many successful speaking tours to Belgium, Canada, Germany, Great Britain, Iran, Pakistan, Spain, Switzerland, and across the USA. Ceremonies including Baccalaureate Lecture, University of LaVerne, La Verne, CA.

Jawaad Khan is a writer and filmmaker out of South Florida, and currently serves as a Literary Editor for the online literary magazine Muslim Youth Musings.

Kamran Anwar is a biological scientist working in the biotechnology industry. After obtaining his PhD from SUNY Downstate Medical Center, he and his family moved to Maryland for post-doctoral fellowship at the NIH. They currently reside in the DC suburbs of Maryland and are very excited to be a part of EPC.

Kashif M. Munir (Past Chair and Category Lead) is Assistant Professor in the Division of Endocrinology at the University of Maryland School of Medicine. He currently sits on the boards of the Financial Independence Group of America, Al-Madina Foundation, and Dar al Islam. He also volunteers for WhyIslam/DC Chapter and reviews books for Fons Vitae publishing. He has been actively involved in various capacities with the EPC and Muslim Youth debate platforms for several years. He currently lives in Howard County with his wife and children.

Kimberly Baqqi is a Biology graduate of Morgan State University and attended Drexel Medical College for post-graduate studies. She is actively involved within the community, including leading a Girl Scout Troop for Muslim girls for the past three years. Her main focus, however, is on homeschooling her three beautiful children and she is most passionate about children and education. She participated three years in a row as a judge for MIST and thoroughly enjoyed the process. She is grateful for the opportunity to positively influence, encourage, and empower our youth, both for MIST and in shaa Allah for EPC in any way she can.

Kulsoom Khan is a former public high-school and middle-school Social Studies teacher in both Baltimore County and DuPage County (Illinois). She is an advocate for the written word! Writing is a personal journey in which an individual thinks deeply, organizes, and express ideas in a thoughtful and powerful manner. Writing is not an easy task! She appreciates when young adults put forth extra thought and effort to produce a quality piece of work for forums like the EPC. As an American Muslim, she sees rhetoric as a powerful tool in helping promote understanding and respect amongst all walks of life in our country and abroad. The yearly EPC is a wonderful opportunity to practice and perfect the art of writing and speaking!

Mahfuz Rahman (EPC 2019 Event Chair) has been coaching/mentoring local youths in essay writing, reviewing and providing feedback on essays. He believes that EPC is a great platform that can significantly contribute to the development of writing skills for our youth. He has previously judged essays in EPC competitions and look forward to seeing our youths succeed at the highest level in EPC!

Maryam Ahmad (EPC 2019 Category Lead) had participated in MYDT as a participant for 5 years and worked with them closely. She has been a judge at the MYDT and judges coordinator. She is a Junior at Zaytuna College, a Liberal Arts College. Maryam is a student at UMUC majoring in English. She had never judged in a competition before, so it would be a new experience for her, one that she hopes to enjoy.

Misba Samiya is a student in University of Maryland College Park. She has judged multimedia/poster sessions in the past.

Musfika Hossain (EPC 2019 Category Lead) is currently an English teacher at Al-Huda School, College Park, MD. She earned her Master's in Education in the Secondary English from the University of Maryland. She has been involved in the Dar-us-Salaam community as a volunteer and teacher of Quranic studies for many years.

Nadia Hasan, MBA, is a social entrepreneur, business planning strategist, government relations professional, nonprofit and human resource manager, public speaker, youth trainer and educator, media contributor, social justice advocate, daughter of a U.S. Marine, and a California girl from Orange County. Nadia is the founder and director of Young Leaders Institute, a youth leadership platform and network connector that empowers youth toward social entrepreneurship

Nishath Fatima is a college student. I have offered my time to judge to help EPC grow and to encourage more and more people to enjoy EPC and learn more about Islam. Nishwath Samiya is currently a student at University of Maryland, College Park. She has been a part of EPC since middle school and believes it is an excellent platform for Muslim youth.

Rehenuma Asmi is an Assistant Professor at Allegheny College in the Department of Philosophy and Religious Studies. She is also affiliated faculty with the Education and International Studies Programs. The EPC essay competition allows me to give back to the Muslim community and to learn about the issues of interest to Muslim youth today. Having youth engage with their faith in critical and analytical ways allows them to investigate and be aware of the richness of the Islamic tradition as well as its implications for modern day society.

Ruqayyah Khan (EPC 2018 Category Lead) is currently pursuing an undergraduate degree at George Washington University. Safiyyah Fatima has been working with youth in the education sector since she was 12. Tutoring, and conducting online reading outreach programs for local non-profit organizations is her specialty. She is also passionate about writing; publishing a WWII veteran's memoir at 19 years old.

Saira Sufi (Chair, Judges Panel and Middle School Category Lead) has over 10 years of professional experience in the event management field. She holds a B.A. in Political Science from the University of Kansas and has her Event Management Certificate from the George Washington University and is currently pursuing her Certified Meeting Planner designation. She has an extensive background in political, nonprofit and government event coordination. Prior to joining Booz Allen Hamilton, Ms. Sufi worked for the Presidential Inauguration Committee as well as the Obama Presidential Campaign. Before joining the campaign, Ms. Sufi worked as the Director of Events for the Center for Social Leadership, focusing on improving the operations of non-profit organizations. Saira offered her time to judge EPC submissions because she feels it is important for Muslim youth to grow spiritually through educational forums. She hopes this will be a learning experience for all involved, particularly in regards to how the Muslim Ummah can be strengthened.

M. Saleet Jafri is a professor and current Chair of the Department of Bioinformatics and Computational Biology at George Mason University. He has published over 40 peer-reviewed journal articles. He holds affiliate appointments at the Center for Biomedical Engineering and Technology at the University of Maryland Baltimore. He received his BS in mathematics from Duke University, a MS in mathematics from the Courant Institute of Mathematical Science at New York University, and a PhD in Biomathematical Sciences from the Mount Sinai School of Medicine/City University of New York.

Sarah Arafat is a senior at Notre Dame of Maryland University majoring in biology to pursue a career in dentistry. She participated in EPC as a contestant for nine consecutive years and plans to stay involved with EPC for years to come in shaa Allah. In addition to being a full- time student, she is the president of her university's Muslim Student Association and Biology Honor Society and also serves as a private Qur'an tutor for children in the Baltimore area. She values diversity, cultural competency, the concept of global citizenship and believes we can all contribute to improving society today.

Sumaiyah Khan works as a Literary Editor for Muslim Youth Musings. "I wanted to get involved with judging EPC because I used to participate in this competition when I was younger, and I have a lot of good memories associated with it. My friends and I gained a lot from our time with EPC, and I think it's important and beneficial for students to practice exploring their thoughts and challenging themselves through writing. EPC provides a good and welcome opportunity for them to practice their skills and improve themselves."

Susan Jenkins (Past Category Lead) works as a Social Science analyst with the US Department of Health and Human Services and has a PhD in Psychology from the University of Michigan. She has served as an EPC judge for almost 10 years and also serves our youth as a Girls Scout leader with Troop 223 through the Islamic Society of Baltimore.

Tasmeea Noor started her career as an architect, and then switched to Information Technology in the mid-1990s. As time permits, she utilizes her technology background for Allah's work. During her student life in Bangladesh, she was an occasional writer for local newspapers. She enjoys active engagement that leads to spiritual growth. She lives in Maryland and mother of two daughters.

Tayaabah Qazi is an educator and a mother of two teenagers, Alhamdullilah. After graduating from UCLA in Neuroscience, she joined the teaching profession and acquired a Teaching Certification in Chemistry and a Masters Degree in Educational Leadership. In addition to teaching, she has also played an integral role as a Vice Principal at a Islamic Schools for three years and as a Educational Program Developer for a year. Currently, she is engaged in homeschooling and providing educational support to homeschooling families by various means, in Baltimore County Area.

Wasif Sikder is a computer engineering student at UMD College Park and was asked to help out with judging. Would love to help!

Yasir Diab is a patent examiner for the USPTO. "I am an avid reader and I am honored to be a part of an initiative that encourages our youth to fine-tune their writing skills and expand their horizons by maintaining a consistent and persistent curious nature. This is my second time judging EPC essays and I hope to available for any service that is required of me."

Yumna Rahman is a college sophomore attending Northern Virginia Community College (NOVA) and pursuing a Computer Science Associate degree. Speaking and writing have always been her greatest passions. She has taken Communications electives and currently working at NOVA's Writing Center. Tutoring at the

Writing Center has given her experience with critiquing essays and speeches alike. Additionally, MAFIQ and EPC hold a very dear place in her heart as she has fond memories of participating in the competition ever since the third grade. She always enjoys reading the thoughts of growing writers and speakers, so she looks forward to this opportunity.

Zahra Ahmed (EPC Organizing Committee Chair and High School Category Lead) is a Family Practitioner practicing at DUS Family Medical Practice in Greenbelt, MD. I became a member of the EPC Committee in 2005 after my eldest daughter participated in the essay competition for the first time. I instantly appreciated such a forum for our youth to be able to express themselves through writing and speech on various topics addressing who they are as Muslims living in America. Our future as Muslims in the West is becoming more and more uncertain. Therefore, I would like to see a panel such as this get to a national level where the voices of our youth can be heard all across the nation, In shaa Allah.

Zahra Aligabi (EPC 2019 Category Lead) is currently pursuing an undergraduate degree at University of Maryland.

Zaakira Ahmed (EPC 2019 Category Lead) is currently pursuing an undergraduate degree at University of Maryland.

APPENDIX E

Glossary of Arabic/Islamic Terminology

Throughout the book, there are several salutations used to show the utmost respect to Allah (swt) as the Creator and to and to the prophets (as) who carried His message. For ease of reading these salutations have been abbreviated as follows.

(as) This salutation is used following the name of any of the prophets. It literally translates as: Alaihis Salaam – Peace be upon him; Alaihas Salaam – Peace be upon her; Alaihumas Salaam – Peace be upon them.

(ra) This salutation is used following the name of any of the Prophet Muhmammad's (Saw) family or immediate companions. It literally translates as: Radi-Allahu 'anhu – May Allah be pleased with him; Radi- Allahu 'anha – May Allah be pleased with her; Radi-Allahu 'anhum – May Allah be pleased with them.

(saw) This salutation is used following the name of the Prophet Muhammad. Although all of the prophets of Allah are highly regarded for their missions and sacrifice, the Prophet Muhammad (saw) holds a higher status as the messenger who received the words of Allah in the form of the Quran, the final and complete guidance for all of mankind. It literally translates as SallAllahu 'alaihi wa salaam – Peace and blessings be upon him.

(swt) This salutation is used following the name of Allah (swt). It technically translates as Subhanahu wa ta'ala – Glory to Him, the Highest.

adhan – The call to prayer made using the human voice rather than a horn or bell, etc.

AH – After Hijrah. The Hijrah, when Prophet Muhammad (Saw) emigrated from Makka to Madinah, signifies the beginning of the Islamic calendar.

ajar – Reward.

akhirah – The Hereafter.

al-Fatihah – The opening chapter or first surah of the Quran.

Alhamdullilah – All praise and thanks is due to Allah.

Allah – The Supreme Creator of the universe and all that exists, whom all Muslims worship. The word Allah is derived from the Arabic word ilah (meaning God). The word "Allah" has no plural or feminine. In contrast, the English word "god" has a plural form (gods) and a feminine form (goddess). The word Allah should always be used in its place.

Arafat – A plain and mountain situated to the north of Makkah. Pilgrims gather here between midday and sunset on the ninth day of Dhul Hijjah to pray for Allah's forgiveness.

Assalaamu Alaikum – Peace be upon you. This is the greeting one should give to his/her fellow Muslims. The reply to this is "Walaikum Salaam" (And upon you be peace).

ayah/ayaat – A verse from the Quran. Literally meaning revelation, it can also describe a piece of evidence or proof, or a sign which leads or directs you to something important.

bismillah – In the Name of Allah.

da'wah – Inviting others to Islam through words or actions.

dhikr – Remembrance of Allah, either through thought or speech.

din/deen – One's religion, faith or way of life.

dua'a – Supplication or prayer to Allah (swt).

dunya – Anything pertaining to this world.

Eid ul-Adha – The Feast of Sacrifice. This Islamic holiday takes place on the 10th day of Dhul Hijjah and commemorates the Prophet Ibrahim's (as) willingness to offer his son Ismail (as) in sacrifice showing an act of obedience to Allah (swt).

Eid ul-Fitr – The Feast of Charity. This Islamic holiday marks the end of Ramadan. It is observed on the 1st day of Shawwal.

fard – Obligatory act, such as the five daily prayers.

fatwa – A legal verdict or opinion given by one or more people well-versed in Islamic law, i.e., a cleric or scholar.

fitnah – Literally a test or trial but generally applies to confusion in the religion, conflicts and strife amongst people.

fitrah – A person's pure state of being before it is corrupted by outside influences. This term is commonly attributed to a child at birth. Because all descendants of Adam (as) made a covenant to Allah (swt) when He asked, "Am I your Rabb?" Everyone answered, Yes! We do testify." Fitrah is a natural instinct. The new reverts to Islam who have just made their shahada or declaration of faith get back to their fitrah.

ghusl – A full ablution, necessary for praying after sexual intercourse or a menstral period, for example, or the act of washing the deceased's body prior to the funeral.

hadith – A verified description of the words or actions of the Prophet Muhammad (saw).

Hajj – The fifth pillar of Islam, Hajj is the pilgrimage to Makkah which every Muslim must take once in their lifetime but only if they are healthy and able to afford it.

halal – Lawful or permissible according to Islamic law, especially regarding food and drink.

haram – Forbidden or prohibited according to Islamic law, especially with regards to food and drink.

hijab – A veil which covers the head worn by Muslim women beyond the age of puberty in the presence of non-related adult males.

hijrah – Literally it means migration and is used to describe the migration of Muslims from an enemy land to a secure place for religious causes, the first Muslims' flight from Makkah to Abyssinia (Ethiopia) and later to Madinah, and the Prophet's migration journey from Makkah to Madinah.

hijri – The Islamic lunar calendar, which began from the Hijrah, is approximately 355 days and comprised of 12 months – Muharram, Safar, Rabi Al-Awwal, Rabi Al- Thani, Jumada Al-Ula, Jumada Al-Thani, Rajab, Sha'ban, Ramadan, Shawwal, Dhul Qa'adah and Dhul Hijjah.

Iblis – The jinn who disobeyed Allah's (swt) order to prostrate to Adam (as) and was expelled from His mercy (also known as Shaytan or Satan).

imam – The leader of any congregational prayer. It is also sometimes used to refer to the head of an Islamic state or an Islamic organization.

iman – Faith, belief.

In shaa Allah – If Allah (swt) wills.

Islam – Derived from the word salam (peace), Islam literally means peace through submission to Allah (swt).

Jahannum – Hellfire.

Jannah – Paradise.

Jannatul Firdaus – The highest level in Paradise.

JazakaAllahu Khairan – May Allah reward you all with good.

Jibreel – Gabriel, the angel through whom Allah (swt) conveyed his words to his prophets. He is also known as Ar Ruh al-Qudus (The Holy Spirit).

jihad – Literally means to struggle or strive and is often incorrectly interpreted as "holy war."

jinn – Beings created from fire, just as angels were created from light and mankind was created from dust. Known in the Western world as spirits, demons, ghosts, etc. Like mankind, Jinn have been granted free will over their actions, therefore some are inclined to do good and some inclined to evil (unlike the angels, who are compelled by Allah (swt) to do his bidding and therefore only do good).

Ka'bah – The structure in Makka to which all Muslims turn to while praying. It was originally built by Adam (as), then subsequently rebuilt by Ibrahim and Ismail (as), then finally cleansed by Prophet Muhammad (saw) and his followers after the pagans of Makkah had used it for their idol worship for hundreds of years.

kafir/kufaar – A disbeliever in Allah (swt) or one who disobeys Him or joins others in worship with Him.

khalifa – The ruler of the Muslim nation. The most honoured khulafaa's were the four who ruled immediately after the death of Prophet Muhammad (saw): Abu Bakr, Umar, Uthman and Ali (ra).

khutba – A sermon given at Jumu'ah (Friday) and Eid prayers.

Madinah – The holy city in present-day Saudi Arabia approximately 250 miles north of Makkah where Prophet Muhammad (saw) emigrated and set up the first Islamic state.

Makkah – The holy city in present-day Saudi Arabia where the Ka'bah is located and where millions of Muslims make Hajj each year.

masjid – Mosque; any place for worship or prayer. The three holiest masaajids are Al Masjid al-Haaram (The Mosque of Sanctuary, located in Makkah), Al Masjid al- Nabawi (The Prophet's Mosque, located in Madinah) and Al Masjid al-Aqsa (The Furthest Mosque, located in Jerusalem).

miraj – The "Night Journey" undertaken by Prophet Muhammad (saw), when he traveled to Jerusalem to the site of the Dome of the Rock (this part of the journey is called "Isra"), and then he ascended to the heavens, met other prophets residing there, and received the command from Allah that all Muslims should pray five times a day (this part of the journey is called "Miraj").

miskeen – Those who are poor.

Muslim – One who fully submits to the commandments of Allah (swt).

qiblah – The direction facing the Ka'bah in Makkah which all Muslims face during prayer.

qiyamah – Resurrection.

Quran – The Holy Book containing all the divine revelations as a final guidance sent to mankind through Prophet Muhammad (saw).

rakah/rakaat – Units of prayers consisting of a series of standing, bowing, sitting and prostrating positions.

Ramadan – The ninth month of the Hijri calendar. It was during this month that the revelation of the Quran began and the bloodless conquest of Makkah occurred.

rasul – A prophet to whom Allah revealed divine texts, i.e. Musa (Moses), Dawud (David), Isa (Jesus) (as) and Muhammad (saw).

salaam – Peace.

salah/salaat – The five obligatory prayers that Muslims must perform every day. These include Fajr (at daybreak), Dhur (at midday), Asr (at late afternoon), Maghrib (at sunset) and Isha (at nightfall). Additional salaat may be performed at different times, e.g. Tahajjud, Ishraq, etc.

sawm – Fasting, i.e. not to eat, or drink, or have sexual relations from dawn (before adhan of Fajr prayer) till the sunset. Fasting during the month of Ramadan is a pillar of faith.

shahadah – A declaration of faith, specifically "Ashadu al la' ilaha illahu, wa ashadu anna Muhammadan 'abduhu wa rasuluhu" (I testify that there are no gods besides Allah and I testify that Muhammad is the servant and the Messenger of Allah).

shariah – Islamic law, derived from the Quran and Sunnah. The laws of Shariah are final and absolute and cannot be changed by human beings.

shaytan – Satan. A devil or any jinn who is inclined to commit evil.

shirk – Associating, invoking or worshipping anyone or anything besides Allah. This is the worst sin a Muslim can commit. In fact, anyone who commits this sin cannot be described as a Muslim.

siwak – A branch or root from the al-Arak tree which is traditionally used as a toothbrush. It contains natural antiseptic and is used by shaving the bark off the end, chewing lightly to soften it, then using it as you would use a toothbrush.

Subhan Allah – Glory be to Allah.

sunnah – The sayings, practices and living habits of the Prophet Muhammad (saw), as recorded in the various hadith collections. Along with the Quran, the sunnah is a source of Islamic law and practice.

surah/suraat – A chapter of the Quran of which there are 114.

taqwa – The love and fear that a Muslim feels for Allah which drives him/her to avoid things that displeases Him.

tawheed – The declaring Allah (swt) to be the only God. It has three aspects: Oneness of the Lordship of Allah (Tauheedd ar-Rububiya), Oneness of worship of Allah (Tauheed al-Uluhia), and Oneness of the name, qualities and the attributes of Allah (Tauheed a-Asma' was-Sifaat).

Wa Alaikum Assalam – And upon you be peace. This is the

proper reply when someone greets you with "Assalaamu Alaikum."

Ummah – A single Muslim community.

wudu – The ritual washing with water which must be performed before every salah prayer.

yateem—Orphan(s).

zakat – A certain fixed proportion of an individual Muslim's wealth and property that is liable as zakat and paid yearly for the benefit of the poor in the Muslim community. The payment of zakat is obligatory as it is one of the five pillars of Islam. Zakat is the major economic means of establishing social and economic justice and leading the Muslim society to prosperity and security.

Zamzam – A sacred well inside the Masjid-al-Haram (the Grand Mosque) in Makkah.